LinkedIn for Business, product pages and Universities

Make your company visible, attract talent and customers.

First Edition 2019

Published by David Martínez Calduch

All rights reserved: David Martínez Calduch

ISBN: 9781793351616

Layout and management for commercialization on Amazon:

Do not go where the road leads.

Go where there is no path and leave a footprint.

- Ralph Waldo Emerson

Acknowledgements

This book is the accumulation of knowledge gathered through study and practice in countless hours, to get to find out what are the right and most effective actions, in every work and project conducted for my company and for the clients, to whom I'm grateful for their confidence in me, and all the knowledge they have provided to me.

David Martínez Calduch

About the Author

David Martínez Calduch

Consultant in Social Selling and Digital Strategist.

Founder of 3 companies, trainer with more than 12000 hours taught and international lecturer.

More than 28 years of professional experience.

Executive MBA ESIC Business and Marketing School - AMBA Accreditation

Book writer: http://amazon.com/author/davidmcalduch

Trainer in companies, business schools and universities in Spain and Latin America. Hootsuite Solution Partner, Hootsuite Ambassador, ECC Certified Evernote Consultant.

Press appearances www.davidmcalduch.com/prensa

More information at:

- **email**: dmartinez@solucionafacil.es
- **LinkedIn**: https://es.linkedin.com/in/davidmcalduch
- **Twitter:** https://twitter.com/davidmcalduch

- **Websites:** https://www.solucionafacil.es
  https://www.davidmcalduch.com
  https://www.socialselling.es/

Introduction

This is the third book in a series called "The Keys of LinkedIn" that are available on Amazon, where I pour out my experience and knowledge, acquired during all these years, using LinkedIn for my own company, and in the projects I develop for my clients.

https://www.lasclavesde.com/linkedin

And on my Amazon author page.

https://www.amazon.com/author/davidmcalduch

This series of books follows a logical process, to apply a methodology of work, and thus get the most out of this fabulous professional platform.

√ **Volume 1 - Create an effective LinkedIn profile to achieve your goals**

In this book, you will see all the planning and creation of a professional profile, which is the cornerstone of all LinkedIn work strategies. How to develop a strategy based on your goals, and how to apply advanced SEO. We will also see security issues and common problems, and how to solve them. Everything you do on LinkedIn is based on the good work that you have done here.

√ **Volume 2 - Get to the right people with LinkedIn**

In this book, I cover the management of the network of contacts, types of strategies to create it, ways to contact, different types of searches, including advanced ones, how to skip the limitations that we can find, techniques of how to invite and communicate, searching to establish communication with the people that interest us. The effectiveness of this book lies mainly in what you have done in volume 1.

√ **Volume 3 - LinkedIn for Business, product pages and Universities**

In this third volume and following the logical order of the series, we will work on the LinkedIn presence from the point of view of companies and universities.

Although it seems like a lie, I still find companies that have not yet created their company page on LinkedIn, or simply do not know what can be done, or have even created a professional profile for your company, something that is prohibited by LinkedIn.

The benefits of having a Company Page on LinkedIn are many, it allows us to tell the story of our company and spread our message to a focused group of professionals.

With a proper content publishing strategy linked to the Employee Advocacy project, we can turn it into a magnet for the generation of Leads.

Companies that publish content at least 20 times a month are capable of ensuring 60% of their followers see 1 post or more.

- LinkedIn

In this book we will deal with what types of content to publish, how, according to what approach we want, and then you will have to develop an entire Content Marketing Plan on LinkedIn for the company.

To design this Content Marketing Plan, the first step that you should define is who or what are the objectives you want to achieve, when, and a value to measure it; we will see some of the objectives that we can set:

√ Attract Talent, the company page has a specific section to post job offers.

√ Unite all the Professional Profiles of the workers and former workers under the Company Page, this I can assure you can help you generate sales.

√ Being able to offer a message in the language of the person who visits us, including different messages by position, sector, etc., offering different products and services in international markets.

√ Improve the SEO positioning of our company / university within LinkedIn and outside, with search engines (Google, Yahoo, Bing, etc...)

√ To be able to create Product Pages, which due to their importance and relevance in the Market, we need them to have their own identity.

√ Have analytics and metrics where we can see the scope we are achieving, what content is more effective, interactions, etc. to make our actions more effective.

√ Carry out advertising campaigns with promoted content.

√ Create a Brand and improve reputation.

√ Launch offers and promotions.

√ Turn the company page into an ally of the commercial team to be faster and more efficient in the generation of Leads.

Considerations to take into account:

√ Creating the company page is free.

√ There is no need to present any official documentation.

√ You only have to register the company if you are the official representative of the company and you have explicit permission from the company to do so.

√ You can not use a Professional Profile (Personal) as a Company Profile.

Sowing the seeds of LinkedIn among professionals and companies since 2009. LinkedIn Conference at the Chamber of Commerce of Castellón with more than 300 entrepreneurs in 2011.

So you can go to the web addresses that are going to appear in the book, and make it easier for you to write them, I will include a QR code in each one, so you can scan them. Below, I include two free applications, one for Android and one for iOS, so you can scan QR codes.

Android	iOS
Kaspersky QR Scanner: Code reader	Kaspersky QR Scanner
https://bit.ly/2FRGcw5	https://apple.co/2DEbAvS

To keep up to date with the important changes that LinkedIn is launching, I've created a page within LinkedIn to keep you updated.

https://www.linkedin.com/company/18582551/

Index

Chapter 1

Why have our company on LinkedIn?

Example is not the main thing in influencing others. It is the only thing.

- Albert Schweitzer

In 2010, LinkedIn had already managed to have a high of 70,000,000 professionals, and that is when it launched the possibility of creating a different professional profile, one specifically for companies, and that same year more than 1,000,000 companies were registered, creating their company profiles. In 2019 there are already 30 million company pages, and 575,000,000 professionals.

Since the launch of the company pages, new functionalities have been incorporated, including a powerful viral content analysis tool.

If you have a company, it is important that you create your company page for the following reasons.

1) Lock the name of your company within LinkedIn in the Companies section, which will remain that way
https://www.linkedin.com/company/soluciona-facil
2) Obtain the SEO position of your company in the search engines, thanks to the power of the domain linkedin.com

3) Allow your employees and former employees to link with your company.
4) Attract Talent.
5) Improve the image of your company.
6) Possibility of creating a marketing plan for specific content for LinkedIn, including Video Marketing.
7) Customer loyalty.
8) Capture of potential clients.
9) Advertising campaigns with great segmentation options.

As you can see, there are a variety of direct and indirect benefits when using the LinkedIn company page.

When faced with launching your company on LinkedIn, it should be a piece within a greater global project, it is not like registering the company on Twitter, or creating the company's website.

The difference with LinkedIn is that it is a professional network; this means that the cornerstone is based on people, and being professional, it is based on your employees, be they managers, department heads and the rest of the employees. So you wish or want, to take them into account so that the project has all its power.

There are companies that make the decision on LinkedIn to do it all on their own, I mean to not take into account their employees, this is the ostrich effect.

This is not going to prevent them from being on LinkedIn, the question we have to ask ourselves is do we want to know what position they have placed and what they do on LinkedIn? Do we want to use the power of LinkedIn even more through our employees?

To do a project of this type in the company, and to plan it well, we have to have 100% of the backing of the management, because we are going to touch certain "sensitivities".

I remember a company where I worked, I was responsible for IT, and I proposed to the management that we should unify the design of the email signatures, basically each one towards the one I wanted and, above all, it was discovered that each one was literally the position that he liked most, including some management. 35 years after the creation of the company, each person was informed about the title of their position.

With this example, I want to tell you, that badly planned, if you want to do it from 0 to 100 within the company, it can be a tsunami. Well planned and executed, can bring us many benefits.

*What you do speaks so loudly, I do not hear
what you say.*

In addition to making the company's page, we should make the professional profiles of the management team, and those that already exist, review them and unify the image, and link all of them with the company page.

From there we can undertake the next phase in various ways:

1) Create a manual of good practices in the use of social networks, with a specific section on LinkedIn, indicating what is the position they must post, and what is the page of the company to be properly linked as employees.

2) Conduct an awareness session about social networks, explain the importance of LinkedIn for the company and for them at a professional level, and explain how to link to the company.

I understand that, if you are going to lead this project, and you are the owner, the only thing I recommend is tact and coordination; if you are responsible for Marketing, you will have to coordinate with the management and with HR, since it is a project that covers many areas.

Another good strategy is of course to link to our salespeople and representatives, here we will have to coordinate with management and sales to see what is the policy that we want to implement.

My experience is that those companies that correctly involve their employees, the results they obtain are worth it. And you must consider that your former employees, will carry the brand of your company in their profiles, even if they no longer work for you.

1.1 Types of pages

1.1.1 Company pages

Here we can see a company page, in this case the company Salesforce.

You can see in the right part a list of "Affiliated pages", which is a functionality that LinkedIn has launched, which allows us to create affiliate company pages, or product/business line pages.

We go to another example of a company, we carry out a search of the company Autodesk.

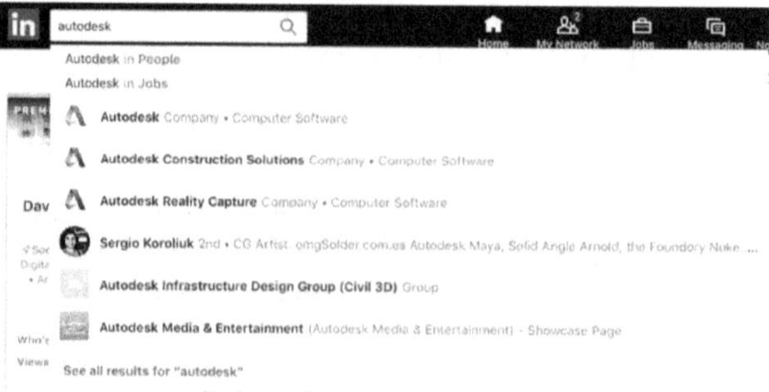

In the search we can see how several "Company" pages appear, with the name Autodesk, the first is the matrix, and the others are acquired companies, or business lines. And the last one that appears is a "Showcase Page", it is a page of a business line.

In the case of universities, we will see that it works exactly the same in this part, we visit the page of the University of Cambridge.

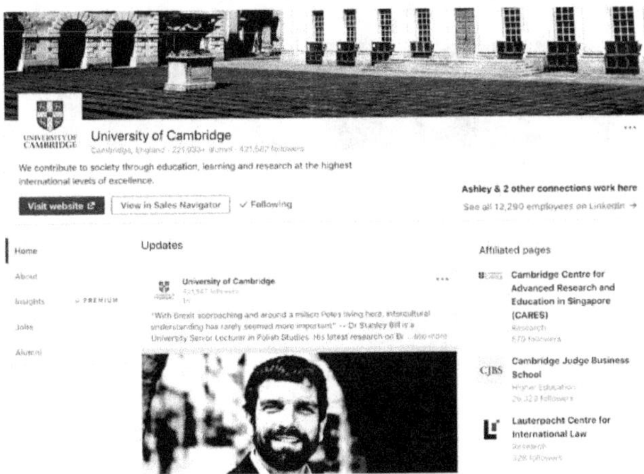

Here we can also see on the right side, the list of "Affiliated pages". And if we do a search of the university, they will appear in the list.

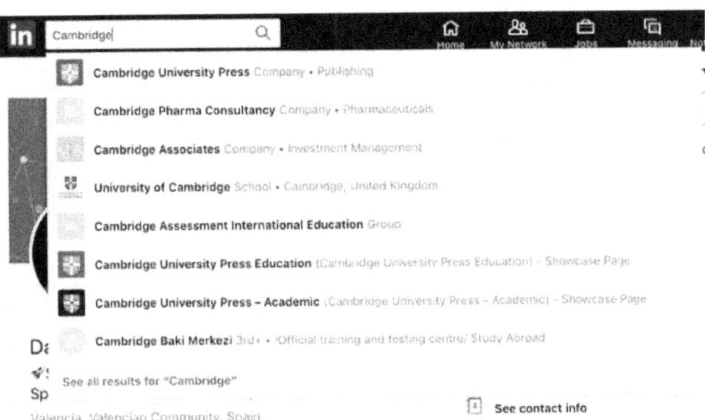

The fourth result is "School", which is the university, the first is the company "Cambridge University Press", the fifth result is a Group, and the sixth and seventh are "Showcase Page" of "Cambridge University Press Education" and "Cambridge University Press - Academic."

So, the first step is to define what strategy we are going to follow, in a first phase, the most advisable thing is to create only one page for our company/university, get used to working with it, and later study the possibility of expanding it with other "Company" or "Showcase Page".

Now let's see the company page of Microsoft.

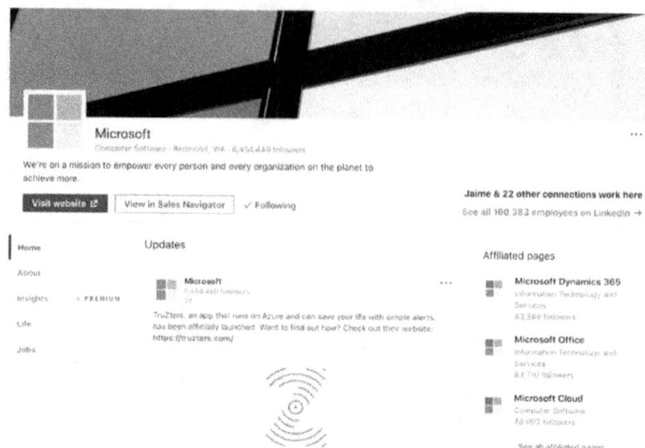

In the part of the right we see the "Affiliated pages" of Microsoft, if we click in the part below "See all affiliated pages", we see a screen with the expanded list.

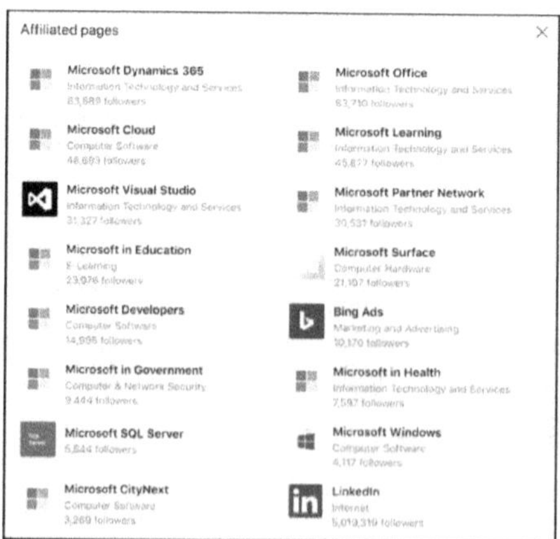

In the case of Microsoft, they have created a different "Showcase Page" for each business line, and below the title of each, it shows to which each business line corresponds "Computer Software", "E-Learning", etc. and below the number of followers of the publications. The goal of creating these "Showcase Pages" is to allow their followers to be up to date only with the business line/product in which they are interested.

If we click on one of them, we see that they are a little different from the company page, a visible difference is the menu on the left, which has fewer options.

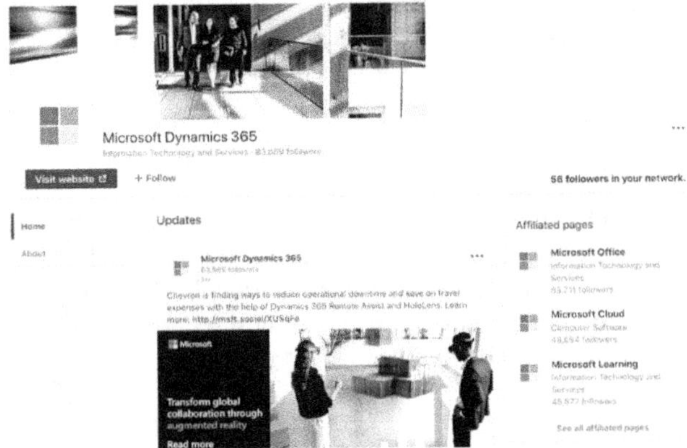

1.2 Success stories

LinkedIn has been a success story with its "Showcase Page" of the marketing solutions division.

https://www.linkedin.com/showcase/linkedin-marketing-solutions/

https://bit.ly/2RW8P1N

Between 2016 and 2018, the LinkedIn Marketing Solutions team has multiplied its followers by 10, exceeding 1,000,000 followers.

LinkedIn publishes a list of which are the best company pages each year, and also indicates why they have been included in the list, indicating what they have done well. We are going to see the pages of companies that have been considered as the best.

1.2.1 Best companies 2018

In the following order from 1 to 10 as published by LinkedIn.

1.2.1.1 Hays

https://www.linkedin.com/company/hays/

2.6 million followers.

The creation of a brand image with leadership through its publications of images with an elegant and consistent appearance, and with genuine thought, taking advantage of the leaders of the company.

1.2.1.2 Schneider Electric

https://www.linkedin.com/company/schneider-electric/

1.3 million followers.

They maintain the brand with their images, a very careful corporate image in all their publications, content focused on achievements and successes for the company and its employees. Also getting to attract the best talent.

1.2.1.3 PTC

https://www.linkedin.com/company/ptc/

160 thousand followers.

They have created a Showcase Page strategy for each line of business, so that they have their own space, which allows them to tailor messages specifically to specific audiences for each one.

1.2.1.4 Teleperformance

https://www.linkedin.com/company/teleperformance/

200 thousand followers.

Publications of bold images containing text, a popular #QuoteOfTheDay campaign, and serial thematic material, including citations and statistics.

1.2.1.5 Cvent

https://www.linkedin.com/company/cvent/

100 thousand followers.

Content with a light and fun tone related to the business, seeking to convey the human side of B2B brands.

1.2.1.6 Grupo Biesse

https://www.linkedin.com/company/biesse/

28 thousand followers.

Publications organized by region, work function, company size, etc. in addition to the appropriate language for each geographical area.

1.2.1.7 Deloitte, North America

https://www.linkedin.com/company/deloitte/

3 million followers.

Content with striking images, beyond stock photos, the use of aesthetically interesting images is sought.

1.2.1.8 Cognixia

https://www.linkedin.com/company/cognixia/

3.7 million followers.

They use their company page for strategic objectives, such as driving registrations for webinars and training sessions.

1.2.1.9 Michael Page

https://www.linkedin.com/company/michael-page/

1.5 million followers

Reduced-size messages to attract visitors, and allow links to further information. A good practice of posts with 150 characters or less.

1.2.1.10 EY

https://www.linkedin.com/company/ernstandyoung/

2.6 million followers.

Native video strategy within LinkedIn, with key figures of the company.

1.3 Benefits of using LinkedIn

To understand the potential that LinkedIn offers, I'm going to show you some data.

- √ 575,000,000 professionals (Volume of users by continents and countries https://bit.ly/2Sdz6rI)

- √ 40% of users visit it every day.
- √ Each year the comments, likes and shares, grow 60%.
- √ All executives of Fortune 500 companies are on LinkedIn.
- √ 45% of all traffic from the RRSS that reaches the company websites, comes from LinkedIn.
- √ 40 million users are decision makers.
- √ 61 million users are senior level influencers.
- √ About 45% of the people who read the articles are in high positions (managers, VPs, Directors and C-level).
- √ Mobile phone sessions grow 57% per year.

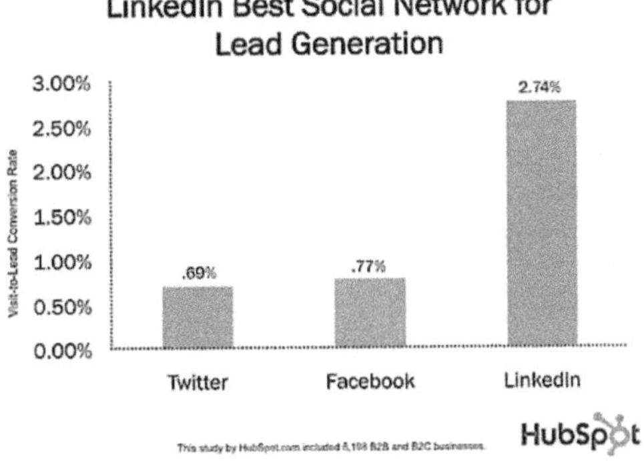

LinkedIn Best Social Network for Lead Generation

- √ LinkedIn is the best place to generate qualified Leads and B2B opportunities.
- √ Companies with complete information get 30% more visits per week.
- √ Companies that publish weekly see a 2x increase in interactions with their content.
- √ 85% of our opportunities are initiated on LinkedIn, Paul Weingarth, Head of Sales, Paypal Australia

Chapter 2

Creation of the company and university page

"Give them quality. It is the best type of advertising."

- Milton Hershey

What we are going to see in this chapter is the creation of the company page, the Showcase Page and the University page.

The company page and the University page, you will see that it is the same process, the difference lies in the type of institution that we are registering, and the functionalities that we will have later.

In the Showcase Page section, first we are going to have to think about what kind of strategy we want to develop, and if this type of page is suitable for our company or not.

The question that we should ask ourselves is, within our company, do we have some products or lines of business that require having their own entity, which will be linked to the company's page. And, on the other hand, will we have much information, news and updates to post on the company's page, and on the Showcase Page pages that we create. If this is not the case, it is better to have only one company page. Unless we can have a very large overload of content creation, the place to concentrate all efforts is on a single page.

2.1 Top

We open the computer and go to LinkedIn.com, in the top menu in the part on the right we have the option "Work".

When clicked, the menu is displayed, and the last option is "Create Company Page +".

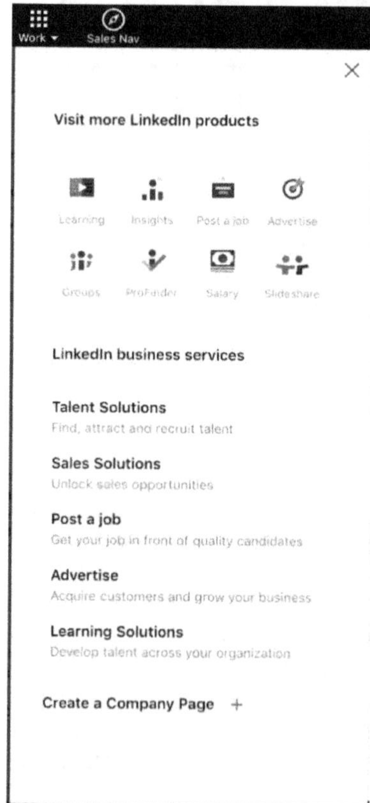

So the wizard appears for the creation of the company or university page. The first step is to select what kind of company we are, the first option is for companies with less than 200 employees, the next is for companies with more than 200 employees, the next option is to create a "Showcase page" and the last one for Educational Institutions "School and Universities".

This is the address to begin

https://www.linkedin.com/company/setup/new/

The first two options are the same screen, with the only difference in the list of the size of the company.

2.2 Creating the company page or Showcase Page

Depending on the size of your company, select option one or two, and when you click, this screen appears. In the part of the left we have the options to configure, and in the part of the right, a preview of how it will be.

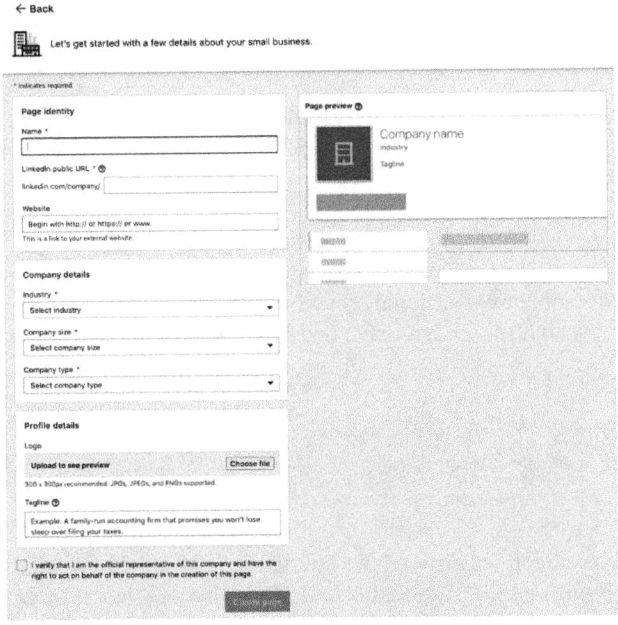

The first part that we have to fill in is the name of the company. You can see that there is a field for the name of the company, and another for the URL that will be the address of our company page. Being a URL special characters and accents, that have the name of your company will not appear here.

* indicates required

Page identity

Name *

LinkedIn public URL * ⑦

linkedin.com/company/

Website

Begin with http:// or https:// or www.

This is a link to your external website.

Thus, in the case of the name of my company "Soluciona Fácil", when writing it, it is as follows.

Name *

Soluciona Fácil

LinkedIn public URL * ⑦

linkedin.com/company/   soluciona-fácil

You can see that, when you type the name with an accent, you also put it in the URL, so in order to have no problem, we must change it to soluciona-facil, leaving the address like this.

https://www.linkedin.com/company/soluciona-facil/

On this screen we only have to write the URL of the company's website, we can write it with http: // Seriously? bad SEO, also in https: // or with www, in my case.

Website

https://www.solucionafacil.es/

This is a link to your external website.

On this screen we only have to write the URL of the company's website, we can write it with http: // Seriously? bad SEO, also in https: // or with www, in my case.

Now we have to fill in the details of the company, select the sector to which your company belongs and the number of employees.

And the third drop-down list, is what type of company it is.

And the third drop-down list is what kind of company it is, we have a public company, self-employment, government agency, non-profit, sole proprietor, private company and association.

The next section, is the most visual part, the logo that we want to appear, the recommended size is 300x300 pixels.

Here you can see the example of my company.

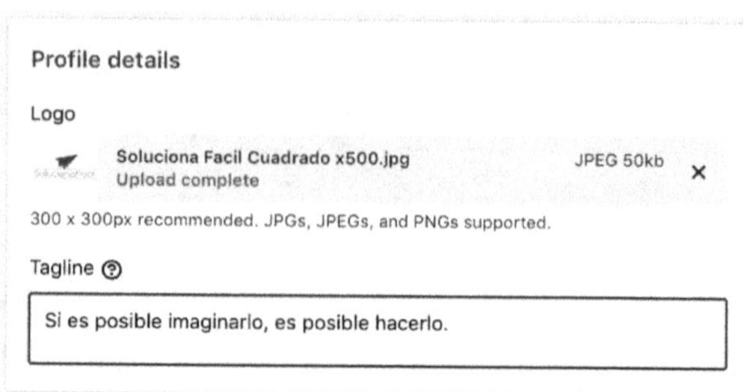

In the "Tagline" we can use it to write the slogan of our company, or explain what we do. And in the part of the right we will have a preview of how you are going to see it.

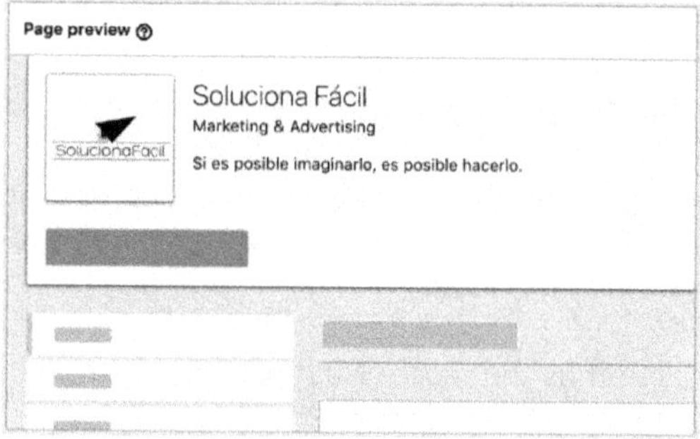

And now only the last box before we can save is to indicate that we are the legal representative, and that we have the permission to create it, if not, you do not create the page of the company, since you will be committing a crime.

If you have permission, activate the box and press save.

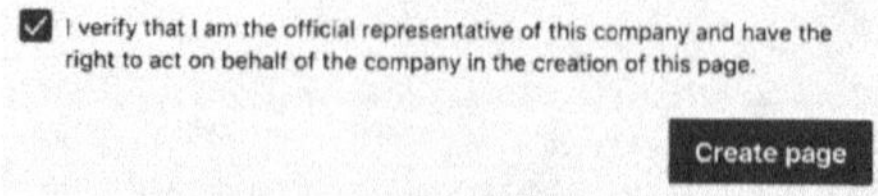

2.3 Creating the educational institution page

We must enter the name of the educational institution, and the address Will automatically appear, written in the URL; if you have written a special character in "Name", it will also appear in the URL and you must remove it so you do not have problems. You can see an example in the previous step.

And the third field is the address of the web page.

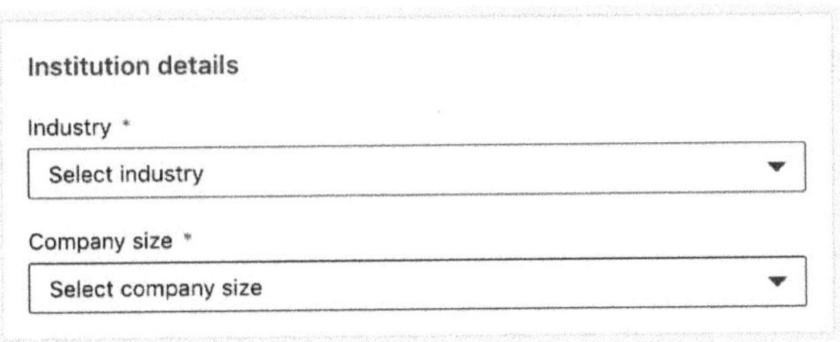

In the next section we have the sector and the number of employees.

Next, we upload the logo in square format, and in the "Tagline" we can explain what we are dedicated to, or the slogan of our institution.

If we are (otherwise do not do it) the legal representative or have express permission to create the page, activate the box and press save.

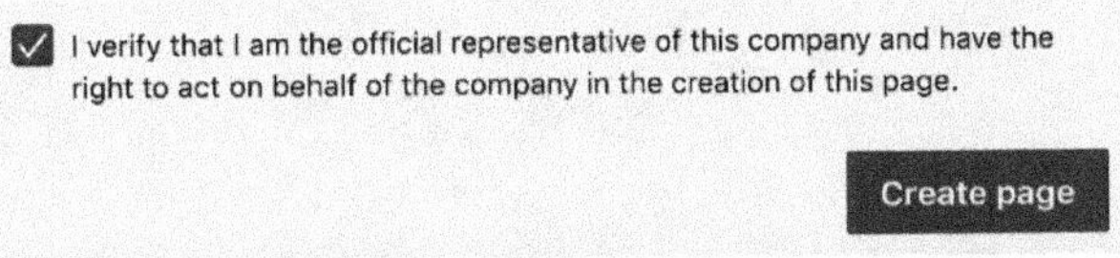

Chapter 3

Configuration of the company page

*"Either write something worth reading or
do something worth writing"*

- Benjamin Franklin.

O nce we have created the company page, Showcase Page or educational institution, we must enter the configuration screen to finish filling in the rest of the options.

We must remember that everything we write in the fields we are going to see, in the end are texts that will be shown in the searches made by users within LinkedIn, and also in the search engines of the Internet, Google, Bing and Yahoo. Once we have the page created and all the data filled, LinkedIn send all the content to be indexed by Internet search engines.

For this reason, it is important to think the keywords related to our company, business, industry and products, we will use when writing the texts. This is because it will have an impact on our SEO (Search Engine Optimization), both on and off LinkedIn.

In this chapter, I will show you examples of companies that are referents in their sectors, so you can see how they are working, visit them (you have the links and QR codes) to get ideas.

3.1 Management of the pages

In the top menu of LinkedIn on the computer, if we click on our photo in the menu "Me", a menu is displayed, with three sections, "Account", "Need help" and the last "Manage", where the pages of companies, Showcase Page and pages of universities appear.

In this menu, it is where the page you have created will appear, click on the name and we will see the page, and we can manage it.

In this menu, it is where the page you have created will now appear, click on the name and we will see the page, where we can manage it.

The screen that we are looking at is the administration screen, you can see the button at the top right to view the page, as seen by the people who visit it.

3.2 Personalization

Being on the Administration page, now we are going to review the different options.

We are in the first option of the "Page" menu, where we will be able to configure the options of our page.

3.2.1 Header image

The largest image that we see with a phrase in the middle is the header image of my company, in the upper right we have an icon with a pencil, and if we click it, a menu appears.

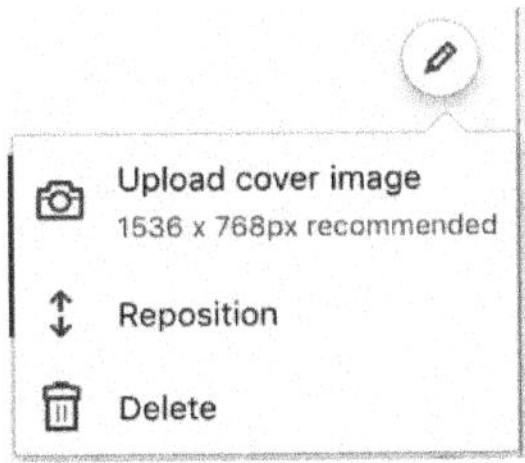

The first option is to load the image we have designed, and the optimal measurements should be 1536x768 pixels, or other higher measures respecting this ratio.

The second option of the menu will allow us to move the image to position it as we want it to look. And the last option is to remove the image we have.

The image that we put here is very important, since we can use it as a billboard, let's see some examples.

https://www.linkedin.com/company/tech-data/

https://www.linkedin.com/company/autodesk/

https://www.linkedin.com/company/mapfre/

https://www.linkedin.com/company/sap/

3.2.1.1 Create our header image

To create the design of the header page we can use the web application www.canva.com, it is also available as an app for Android and iOS.

iOS

Android

For the creation of the header image, the best way to do it is to contact your Marketing Department, so that they are responsible for the design, since they must be consistent with the company's style.

In case you have to do it, you can use this fabulous tool and I will show you how you can do it.

1) Go to canva.com, if you are not registered, it's free.
2) When entering the design assistant, we look for or write LinkedIn, and find a specific one for LinkedIn.

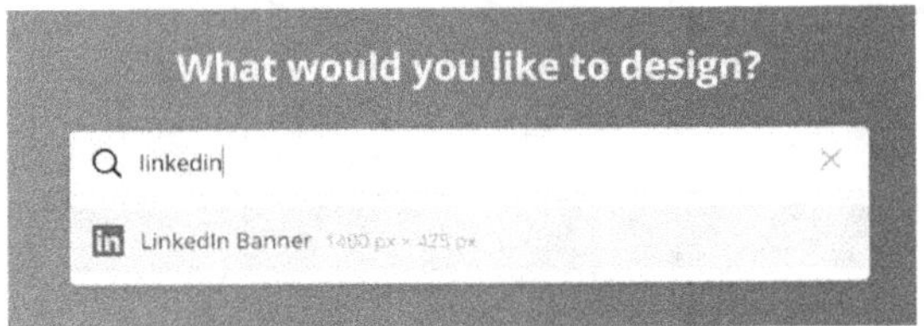

3) We select it by clicking, and the design editor will open and in the left part we will see already created designs. What you have to do now, is to look for the one that looks most like the one you would like to make, so you can use it and make the least amount of changes possible.

4) I'm going to use the second to show you the example.

5) The first thing we are going to do is change the dimensions so they are exactly the ones we need which are 1536x768 pixels. To do so, in the upper left corner we have the "Resize" menu".

6) We select the "Custom dimensions" option, we put in the measurements and press the button "Copy & Resize".

7) In the left part we click on "Uploads" to upload an image of our computer, which is the one we are going to use. If you want to look for an image to use, you can visit these image websites.

    a.   www.pixabay.com
    b.   www.pexels.com
    c.   www.unplash.com

8) Once you have the image located and downloaded to your computer, inside "Uploads", you have a button to upload the image to Canva so you can use it.

9) We click on the image of the typewriter that we have in the design and delete it.

10) Now we click on the left part of the screen, where we see the image that we have loaded and it will appear in the middle of the design, now we stretch it until it occupies the whole design.

11) In my case, being such a clear image, the white text is not visible.

12) So we click in the middle of the text and at the top we change it to black, in the subtitle we do the same, and we move them to the left.

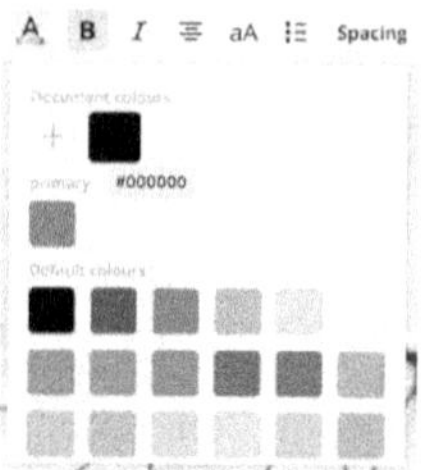

13) And that's how the design is done.

14) At the top, we can change the name of the design, which will be the name of the file when we download it.

15) Now we can just download it in PNG format to have it in maximum quality, and we can put it on our company page. We select the option "Download".

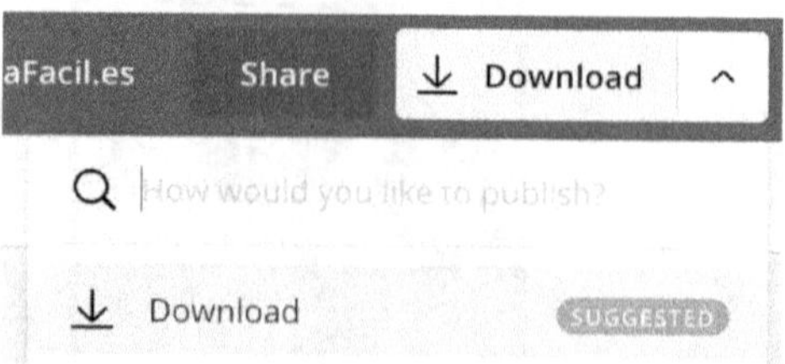

16) And this screen appears for me to be able to download it in PNG to our computer.

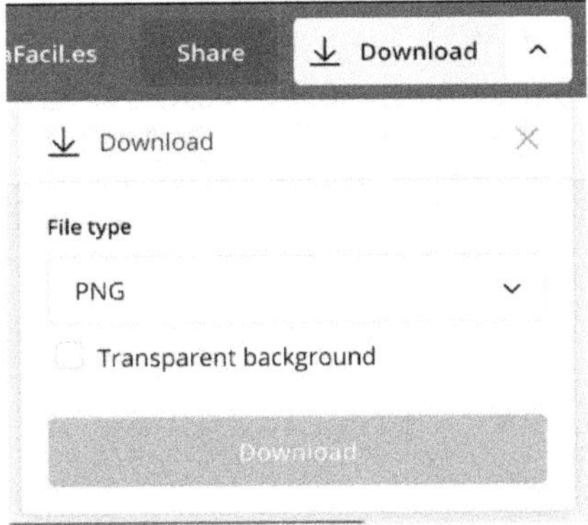

When designing, you must take into account that you have to follow the current graphic image of the company, colors, typography, etc.

3.3 Header

In the part of the right we have a pencil-shaped button, when clicking, this screen will be shown, with all the configuration options.

In the left part, you will see that we have three main sections, "Header", "About" and "Manage languages". Now we are in the first section "Header", where we have two options in the menu, "Page info" and "Buttons".

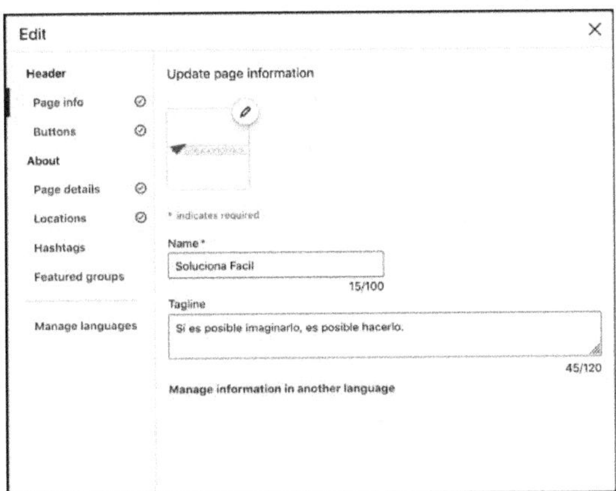

3.3.1 Page info

In the left part, you will see that we have three main sections, "Header", "About" and "Manage languages". Now we are in the first section "Header", where we have two options in the menu, "Page info" and "Buttons".

Update page information

* indicates required

Name *

Soluciona Facil

15/100

Tagline

Si es posible imaginarlo, es posible hacerlo.

45/120

Manage information in another language

The first option with a pencil is to change the icon of the company.

The second field is the name of the company / university that you have placed.

And the third is a slogan that we have written.

In all the screens that we are going to see, in the end, you will always see an option "Manage information in another language", to make all the information in other languages.

3.3.2 Buttons

An option that the company page now incorporates is the Showcase page and educational institutions, is the addition of a button with a URL.

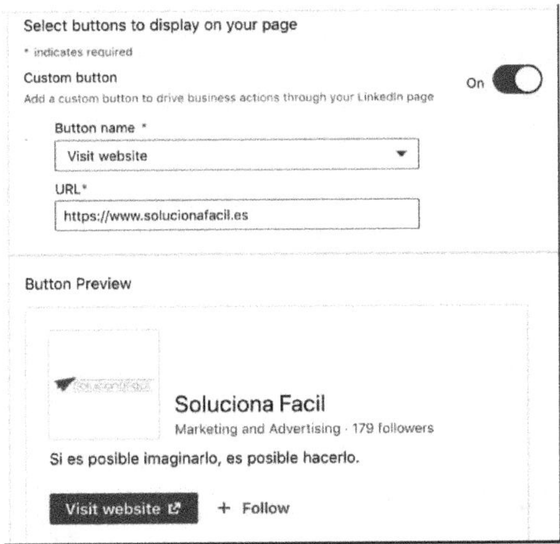

The first option is on the top right, which is to activate or deactivate the button. If you already had the company page created before they launched this option during 2018, it will be disabled. If you want to use it, you must come to this screen, activate this option and configure it.

Here we can see the options that we can select, which is the name that will appear on the button.

Then we have the "URL" field where we write our URL, it is better that you try the address in the browser, and do copy and paste, to avoid errors and that does not work.

And at the bottom, we see how the button is.

3.4 About

The next section is "About", which is the data about our company, and inside we have the sections "Page details", "Locations", "Hashtags" and "Featured groups".

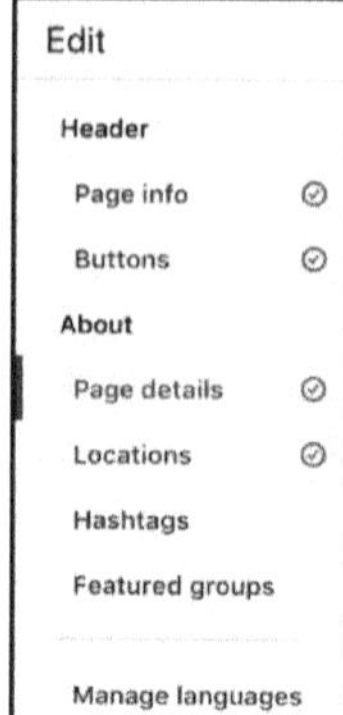

3.4.1 Page details

In this section we will provide more information about our company, the first field is the "Description", where we can write up to 2000 characters. This is the text that the people who visit our company page read after clicking, in the "About" section.

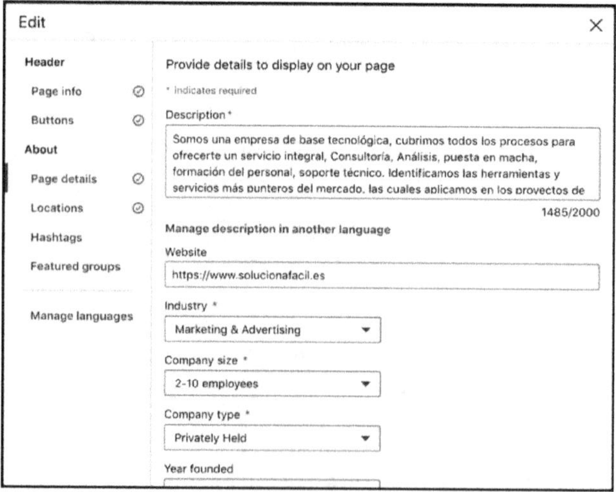

One way to write that text is to use the one you already have on your website, on the About page or who we are, our history, or what we do.

The objective that this text should fulfill is that those who read it understand what your company does, what kind of product or service you are dealing with in your Showcase Page or which sector it is focused in, and in your educational institution, what type of education and training you do. You must remember that it is very important to think in terms of SEO and keywords in which you want to position yourself.

The rest of the fields that appear in this screen are those that we had already introduced when creating the page, and here you can modify them in case it is necessary. The last two fields that the screen did not have before available are the first is the year in which the company was founded.

And the last field of this screen is that of the "Specialties".

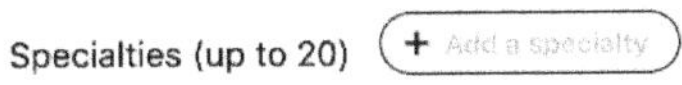

The maximum that we can enter is 20, this section is very important and you should fill it out; if you do not think of 20 initially, put at least between 8 and 10. You should consider these "Specialties" as powerful keyworks for your SEO, since they will help you position your company page, both on and off LinkedIn. So carefully consider the words you want to put.

At the time of writing, no assistants appear to advise you to look up words. Other information we must take into account, that we will see later with the possibility of working in several languages on the company page, is that these "Specialties" are 20 unique words, there are 20 for each language, only for the language established by default. Its operation in this part is equal to the "Skills" of the professional profile.

3.4.2 Locations

This section is where we will be able to specify the address of our headquarters, and all the offices or stores we have.

Add or manage a list of your locations

+ Add a location

Address	Location name	Actions
Spain	(Primary)	✎

At the top we have the button to add new addresses "+ Add a location", and clicking it makes this screen appear.

Add location

* indicates required

Country *

Select a country ▼

Street address

Apt, suite, etc.

City *

State/Province/Region *   Zip/Postal code *

Location name

☐ Set as default location

The first thing we have to do is select the Country, and so when we type in the address, we already have a list of addresses, to indicate which is ours, so after entering the company's page, people can see the map of that location.

This is what the address of the University of Cambridge looks like, you can see the map on the right.

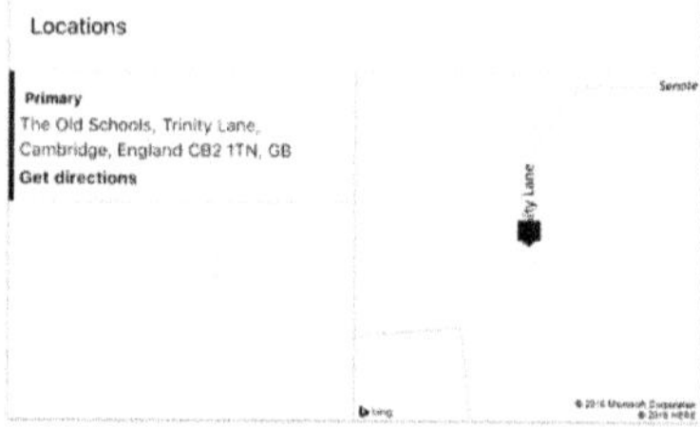

In this example we see the addresses that Autodesk has put on its company page.

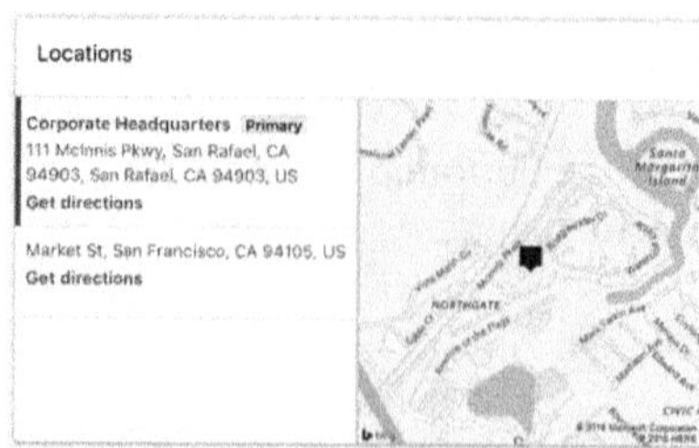

It is possible that, in certain businesses, the option of putting the address is not the best idea, we will see some cases of this.

In the case of an autonomous / self-employed person, who works on their own, and that performs work in their clients' own facilities.

If you are a Startup, it may be that at the moment you do not want to establish the address of your offices, or you can put the address of the accelerator where you are. Another option is to put the address of the coworking space where you work.

3.4.3 Hashtags

In the "Hashtags" section we can define three hashtags.

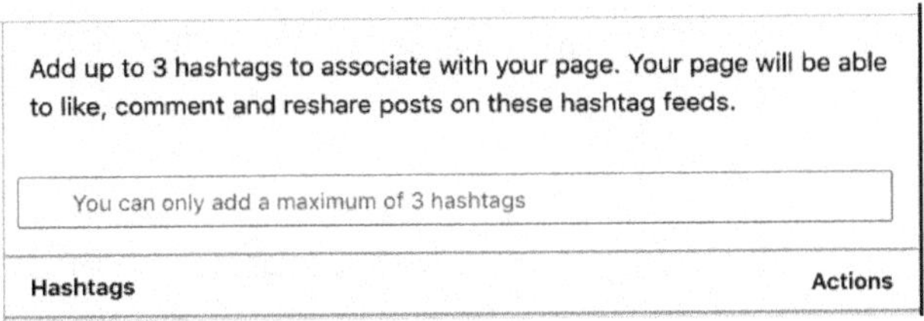

This will allow people to interact with the posts on our company page, to reuse and share with these hashtags.

3.4.4 Featured groups

In this option we can indicate groups that we manage.

Here we see the example of Autodesk's groups.

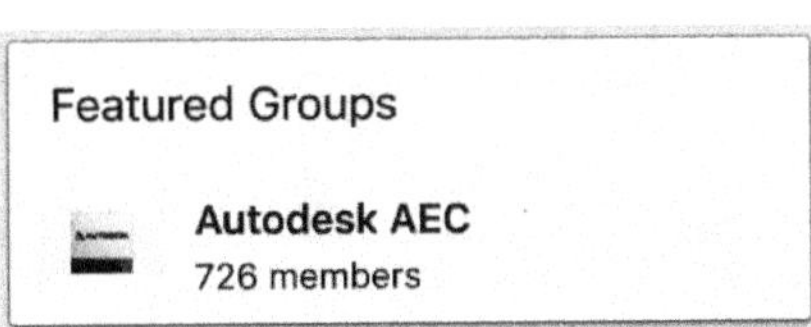

The use of groups within the strategy of the company, planned in a correct way, can be very useful.

3.5 Multi language

The last option of this screen is "Manage languages", which in the same way that we can have our professional profile in several languages, we can do the same with the company profile.

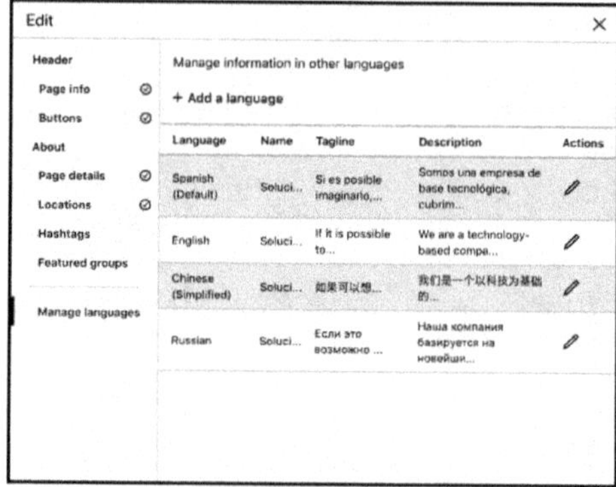

We can see the case of "Soluciona Facil" where we have created the profile of the company's page in 4 languages, Spanish, English, Chinese and Russian. And you can set which language is to show by default.

If your business works internationally, this is a very interesting option, imagine that a person from China visits my profile, automatically LinkedIn will show them the page of my company in Chinese, likewise in Russian, etc. So, we should create the company page in the language of the markets where we work.

Another advantage is that it is possible that we do not sell all our products / services portfolio in one of the countries, then in that language we only talk about what we offer for that market. When we enter to create another language, it will not allow us to modify all the data that we have configured, since many are common.

As you can see in this example, the fields that we will be able to customize in each language are:

√ Company name
√ Tagline
√ Description

As you can see the "Specialties" are not different by language.

3.2 Checking our page

Once our page is created, now what we have to do is check if everything is correct, so we must see how the people who visit it will see it.

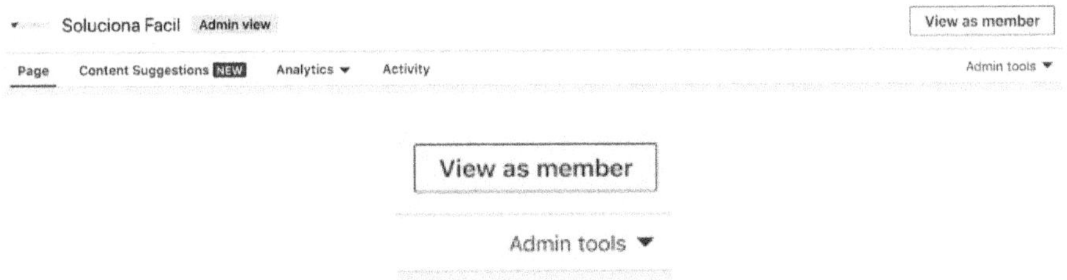

When on our company page, in the upper right, we have the "View as member" button, which will show us the page as the people who visit it will see it.

And to return to the administration page, now we will see the button to return to the area of the administrators.

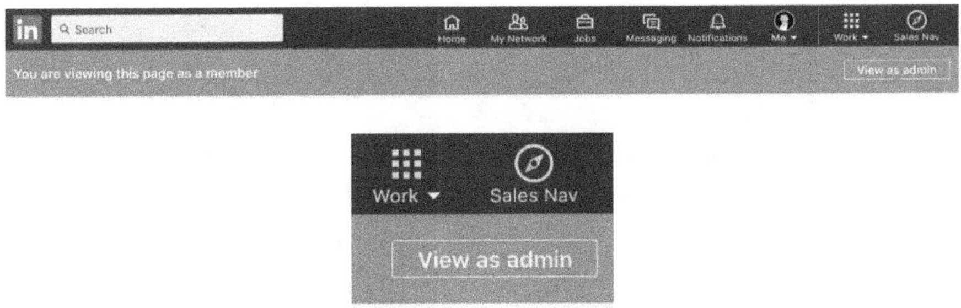

What we have to do now, is to enter this option and:

√ Read all texts again to see if they are correct
√ Test the button that we have configured to confirm that the address works.
√ Check that the logo looks good.

√   Check that the header image looks good.

And all this must be done on the computer and from the LinkedIn application for Smartphone, especially the logo and the header image.

Chapter 4

Administration of the page and posts

Fom the administration screen we will be able to manage all the options offered by the company pages, Showcase Pages and pages of educational institutions. The permission level, posts, etc.

In the top menu, in the left section, we can see that we are on the screen as administrator because the title "Admin view" appears with a gray background.

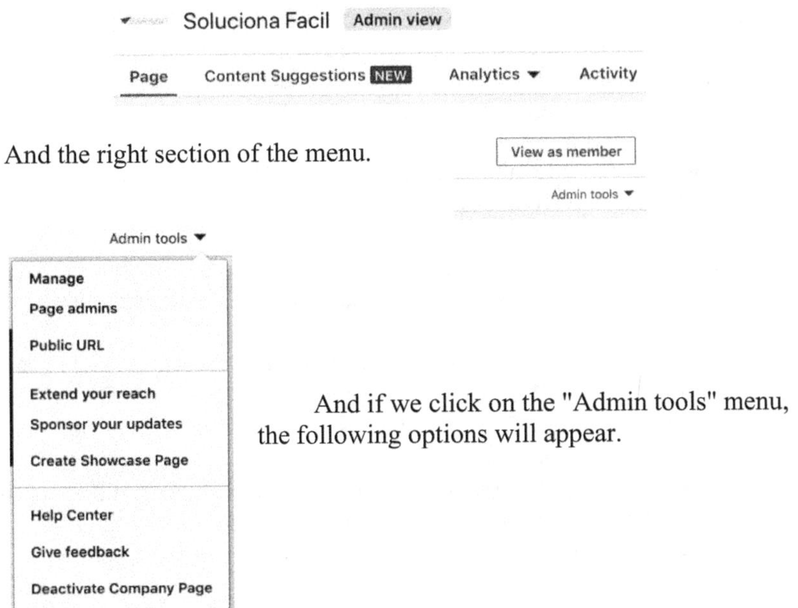

And the right section of the menu.

And if we click on the "Admin tools" menu, the following options will appear.

4.1 Manage

4.1.1 Page admins

This option is the first one that you should configure, which is where we can add other people, to help us in certain tasks of the company page.

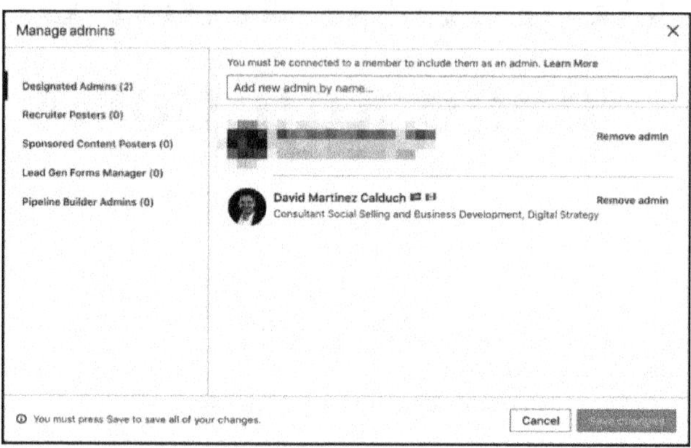

My advice is that there should not be just a single person as Administrator of the company's page, because, if there is a problem with that person's LinkedIn account, nobody will be able to manage or post on the company's page, so it is recommended that at least two administrators be assigned.

In small companies, one may be the person who will manage the company's page, and another Administrator may be the owner, Marketing Director, ICT Director, Financial Director, even if they are not going to touch anything on the page, nor post on it. In this way, we make sure that we can always access the company's page with another professional profile.

If we are the ones that we are going to add other people to add them as Administrators, we can only do it if they are our contacts in LinkedIn level 1.

In addition to adding a person as administrator, you can also assign what kind of tasks you can do or not, having these types of Administrator available:

- Designated Admins, which can change the design and make posts.
- Recruiter Posters, which can post job offers.
- Sponsored Content Posters, which can carry out advertising campaigns.
- Lead Gen Forms Manager, those who can manage the Lead capturing forms within LinkedIn, and manage the data obtained.
- Pipeline Builder Admins, those who can create Landing Pages.

4.1.2 Public URL

In this option we can change the URL of the company page, it is best not to change the address of the company page.

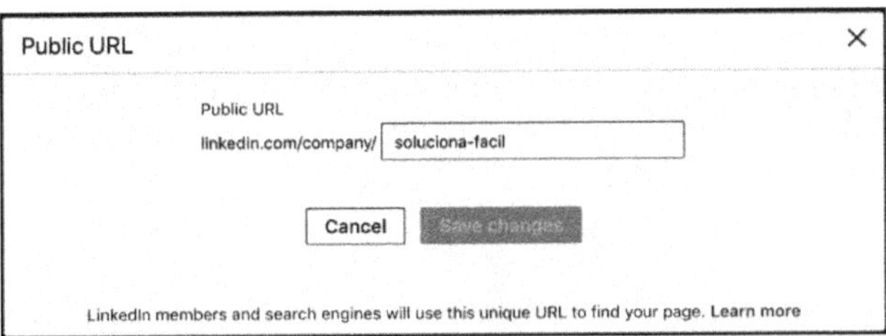

You must keep in mind that if you change the name of the company for any reason, the URL does not change, you must do it manually. But changing the address has the problem that the old URL does not redirect to the new URL.

On the company page, you have a second address that can only be viewed by administrators, each company page has a number, so my page is seen as

https://www.linkedin.com/company/soluciona-facil

It is also https://www.linkedin.com/company/591719 and in fact this address leads to the other, although it will change the name to the company in the URL.

At the level of SEO and internet search engines, when making the change to the URL, LinkedIn will send the change to the search engines, but this change will take a few weeks to be updated in their databases and the results they show.

The previous name of your company in the URL, that is, your old URL will be blocked for 365 days, so during that time, no one can create a company page with that URL.

Once you have changed the address, it remains blocked for 30 days without being able to modify it.

LinkedIn penalizes deception attempts or ambiguous addresses, such as when the name and URL do not match, or making certain changes such as "the" to "them", etc.

4.2 Page

The first option that appears is "Page", where we can enter having made the configuration and personalization of our page, that we saw in the previous chapter.

In addition, we can see a summary of the statistics of our page, if we click on any of the %, it will send us directly to the corresponding screen with the statistics to see the evolution.

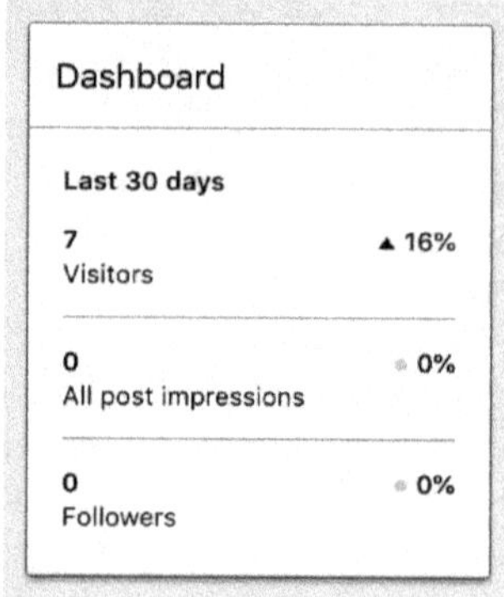

Also on this screen is also where we are going to make all the posts that will appear on our company page.

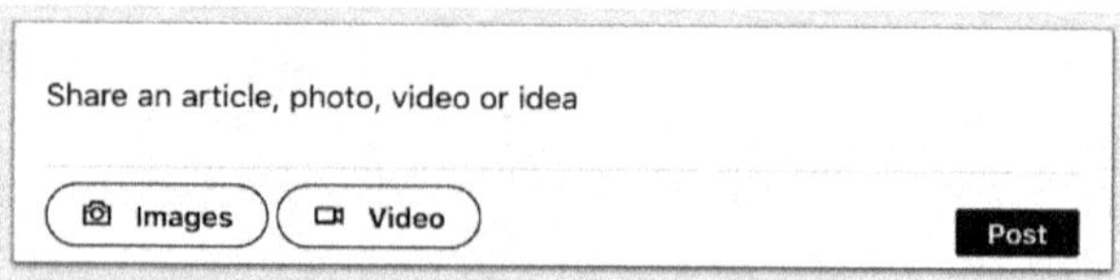

4.2.1 Post from the computer

This section has undergone a lot of remodeling, to allow us to segment what we want to post in our posts in an efficient way, based on the user base that follow our page.

Here we will not suffer the famous limitations of scope that Facebook makes in company pages.

By clicking on the area to write, we will automatically see a screen like this.

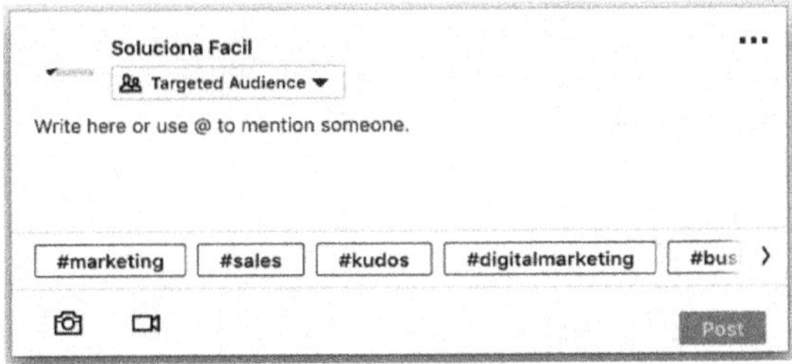

From the company page, the post options are different from those we can do from our professional profile through the home page.

4.2.1.1 Post links

The way to publish a link to an external source properly is the following:

1. We look for the news that we are going to post

2. We click on the news and copy the URL
3. We return to the page's posting screen and paste it, which will generate the preview of the post.

4. As the preview has already been generated, we no longer need to have the URL written, since clicking on the image will go directly to the news, so we delete the URL of the text, and write a sentence.

If the preview of the link has not been generated, it is because you must have a problem in setting the predefined image for the post, if it is your own web address, you should contact the Content Marketing Manager to discuss it and solve it.

Another solution is that once the image has been loaded and it shows nothing, at the top left you will see an icon of a photo camera appear, with this icon you can upload the image you want to be published with your link.

5. And now we could publish this news on our company page, but better to apply the following two points below.

4.2.1.2 Mentions

A very good technique to get interactions is to mention companies and professionals, as long as they make sense within the publications we make. In the example that concerns us, we will make the corresponding mentions.

What we do is delete the word "LinkedIn" we have written and instead we write @ and little by little we write LinkedIn, and this list will appear.

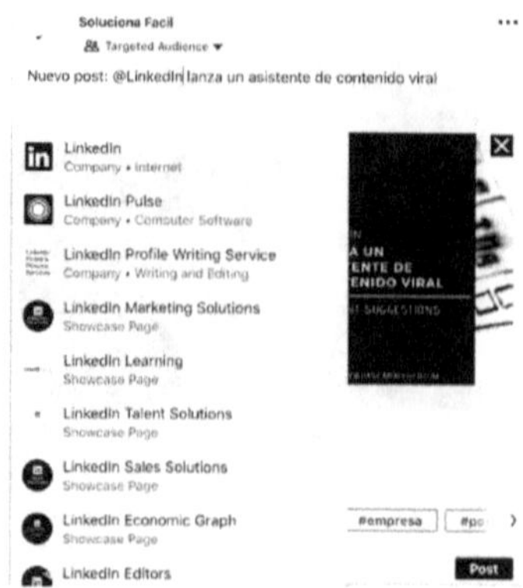

The first result that appears in the list is LinkedIn, we click to select it and we will see how the text turns black, we have linked the text LinkedIn with your company page, like this:

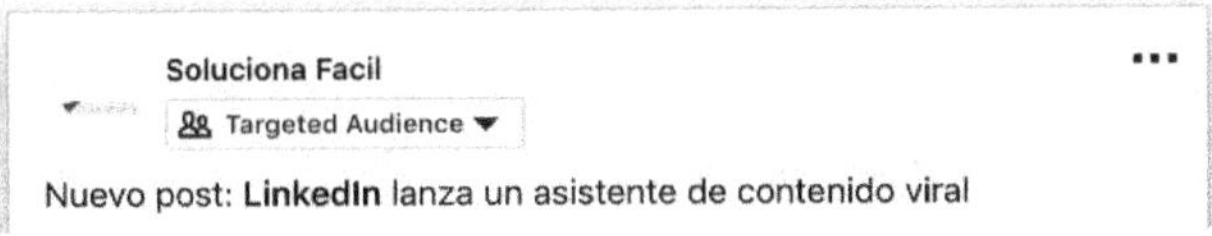

And now I will do the same, naming myself as the author so you can see the example, follow the same steps, @ and then write the name of the person we want to name.

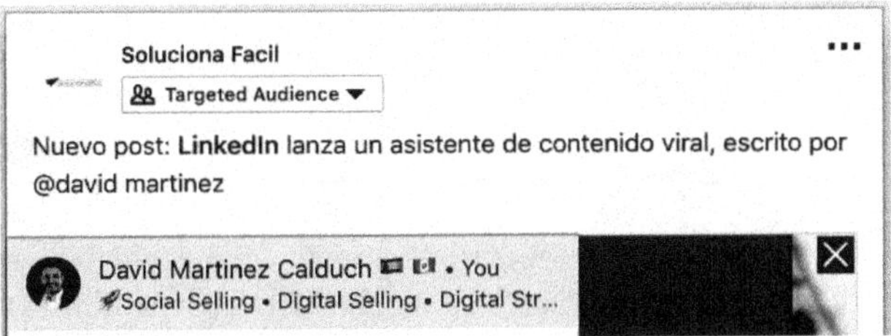

And from the list we click and we will see how the name appears in bold, which means that your profile is linked.

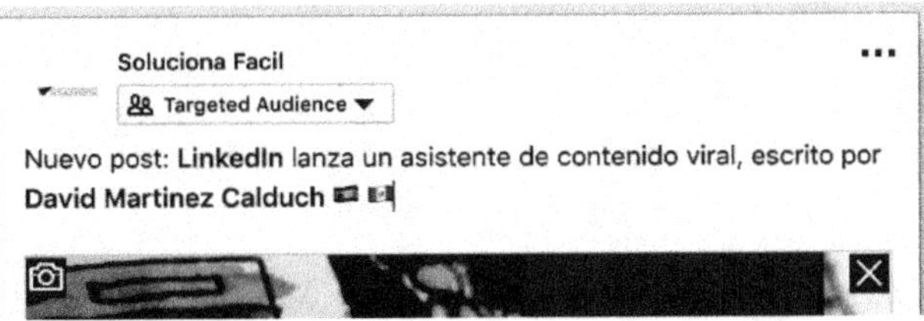

Keep in mind, that this option that we are seeing is very powerful, because when we click publish, the Community Manager who manages the LinkedIn company page will be notified, his company has been named in a post, and can see what the post is, in case they want to interact in it.

When naming people, they receive a notification on their LinkedIn, desktop version and Smartphone application. It is a functionality, that well used has great power.

4.2.1.3 The use of hashtags

The publications we make from our company page, Showcase Page or from our educational institution, unfortunately, will only be seen by those people who are followers of our company page.

So, the way to reach more professionals, who still do not follow our company, is to reach them through common interests, i.e., if we publish content on Big Data, it would be interesting if our content could reach people interested in this type of information.

The way to do it is through the use of hashtags, which unite us with other people who are following those same issues. Initially it is always better to use hashtags that are already being used by other professionals on LinkedIn, to be able to include our content within those content threads under those hashtags, since, if we use our own hashtags and nobody else uses them, nobody will see them.

In the lower part of the publications screen, we see that the hashtags assistant appears, here there are recommendations of hashtags depending on what we have written, the latest hashtags we have used, and hashtags related to the hashtags we are using within this post.

To put the hashtags within our post, it is best to do it at the end, and put at least 5 to position our content.

Following the strategy that we have defined, we must try to use those three hashtags that we have defined in the configuration page, and where we have indicated that they are the topics we are dealing with.

One way to put the hashtags is to simply click on the hashtag that we have in the list and see what interests us.

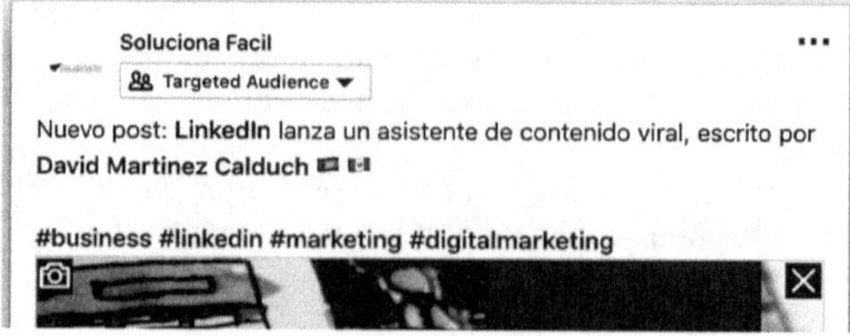

Another way to write the hashtags is to do it manually, and have the hashtags assistant appear, to tell us which ones are being used. We write the symbol # and little by little we write the word, so that the list of recommended hashtags comes out, and we click on the one we want to use.

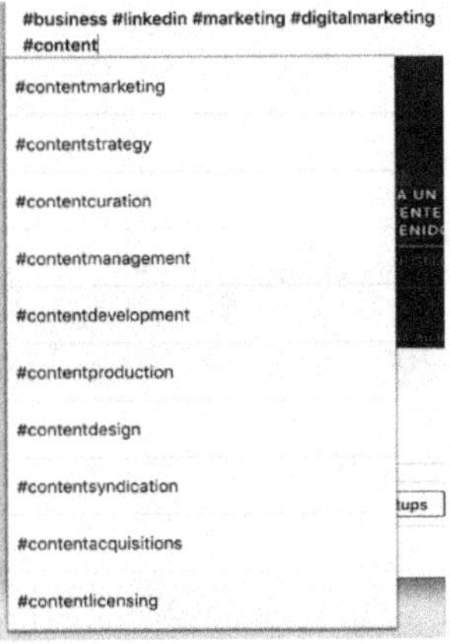

4.2.1.4 Posting images

4.2.1.4.1 Post an image

Another option we can do is to post photos or graphs that we have created.

We go to the publications screen on the company page, and click on the "Image" button.

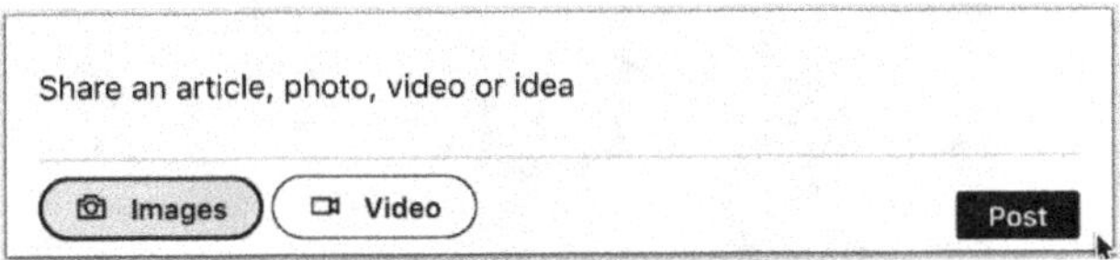

The file explorer will open, we search for the image, select it and press accept.

And we will upload the image and we will see how the post will look.

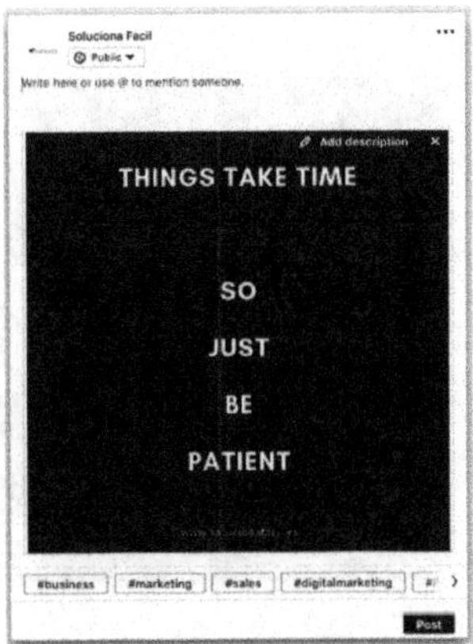

Now what we should do, is to define the HTML tag called ALT, or as it is usually called, alternative text. If we do this, it will help us in the SEO positioning of this post, to do it we just have to press the "Add description" button that we have in the upper right part of the image that we have loaded.

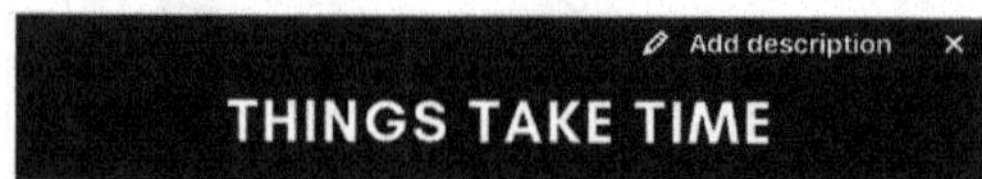

By clicking on the pencil icon or the text next to it, this screen will appear where we can write the text, the maximum is 120 characters.

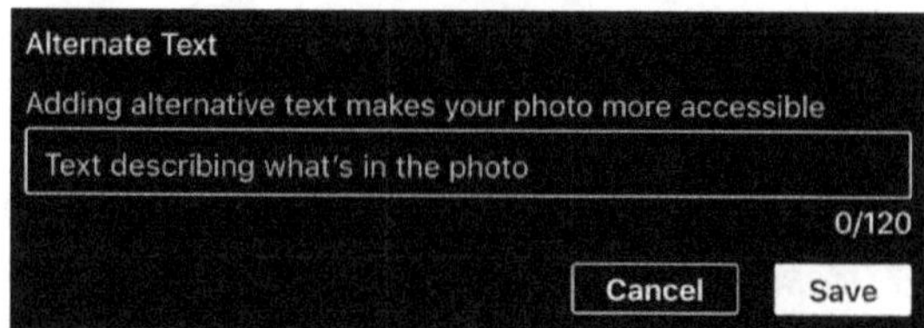

In my case, I write the same text that appears written inside the image, like this.

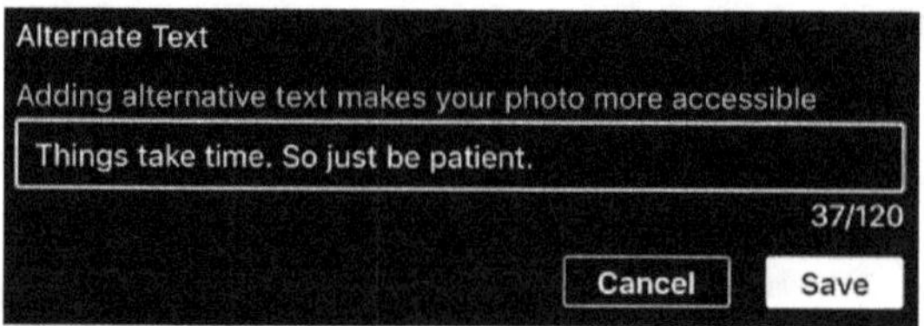

And when posting the image with the alternative text, it looks like this, as you can see, the alternative text is not visible to the naked eye, but it does show up in the searches that people do.

You can see that, at the top of the post, my name appears, as the person who has made this post. We can see this because we are on the Administrator's screen, so we can know which team person has published each of the posts.

If we go to the view that people who visit our company page see, they only see that it has been published by our company, but they do not see the name of the person on our team.

It is possible that when you go to see how people who visit your page will see the post, (you must click the top right button for the "View as member" screen), that the post does not appear. You must wait a few moments until it appears, although when you go to your Administrator screen, it is actually published.

4.2.1.4.2 Posting multiple images

We can also publish several images in the same post, so LinkedIn creates a gallery of images, it's the same as we've seen so far, with the only difference that, instead of selecting a single image, you select several images, here's an example of how the post looks.

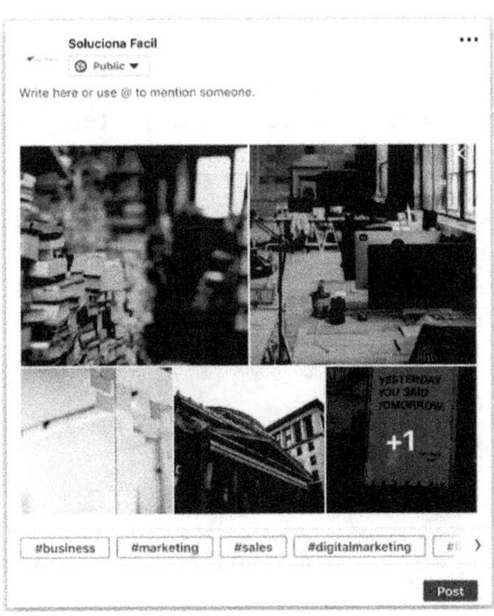

But you can see that we do not have the option for the alternative text.

4.2.1.5 Posting videos

To post videos from our computer on our company page, we click on the "Video" button and select the video we are going to post.

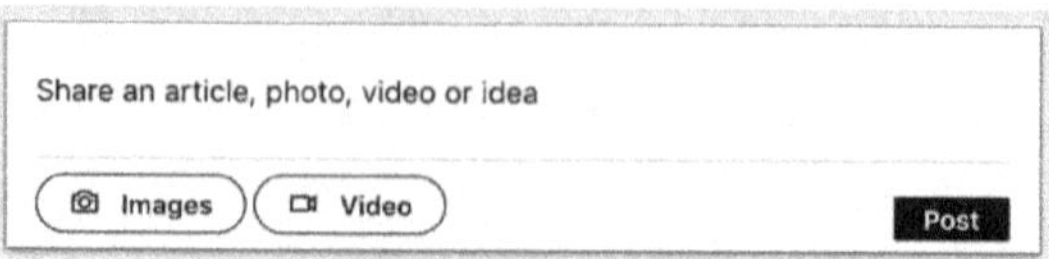

LinkedIn uploads the video, and once it is ready to be published, you will see the video preview.

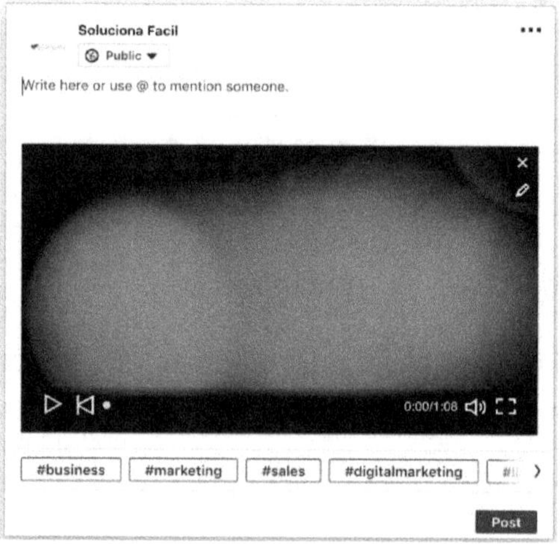

You can see, that inside the preview of the video, in the upper right part, we have an icon with a pencil, when we click this screen will appear.

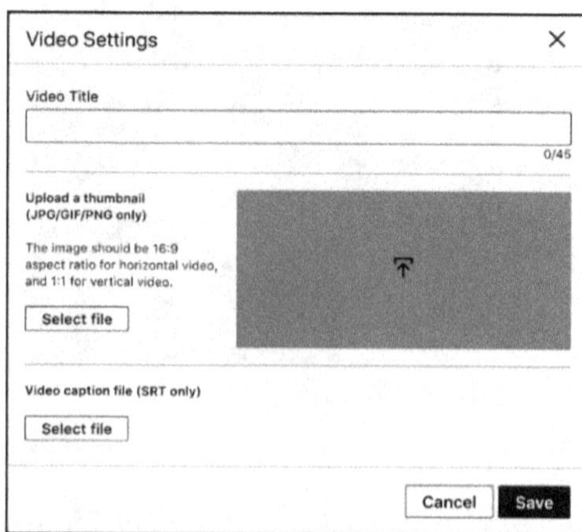

In this screen, we can define a title for the video, load an image, so that it is the image that is seen before putting the video in motion, and to load subtitles.

The idea of loading subtitles is a very good idea, the reason is that we are in a professional environment, and many professionals have the volume of multimedia content playback muted in their work Smartphones. This means that, when viewing the posts on their LinkedIn wall, the videos are played, but they do not hear anything, so putting subtitles solves the problem. Another advantage of subtitles is for people who do not know the language they are listening to, which will help them to better understand what is being explained.

4.2.2 Posting from the Smartphone

In 2019 LinkedIn has introduced the ability to publish to our company page on the Smartphone application if we have administrator permissions.

4.2.2.1 Posting screen

Now we go to the LinkedIn application for Smartphone, if you look for the button where we can go to our company page, at the moment it does not exist. So we have to get to the page of our company, a simple and quick way to do it, is to search for it.

We click on LinkedIn's global search engine, and write the name of our company, in my case I search for "Soluciona Facil" and I see these results.

And when entering our company page, if we are administrators, in the bottom right, we will see a blue round button with the symbol of a pencil.

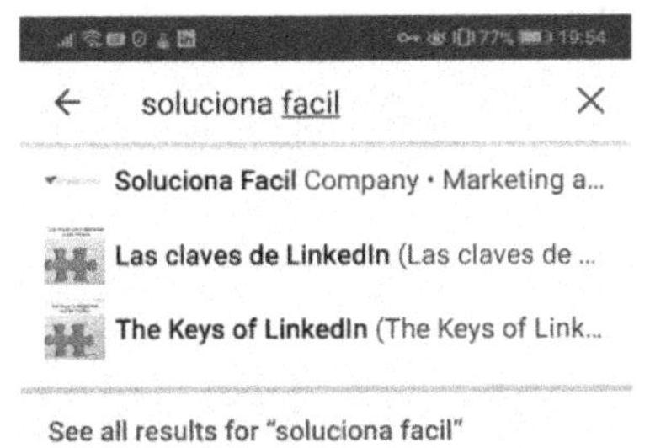

The posting screen is basically the same as the computer screen, we have a zone to write, the assistant appears with the hashtags that are being used more or "Trending".

And below we have an @ icon which is to name companies and professionals, the icon of a photo camera to post photos, and the icon of a video camera to post videos.

And now let's see how it works.

4.2.2.2 Post a link

The only way that LinkedIn currently allows us to post a link from our company page is to follow exactly the same steps we have taken on the computer.

1) We open the browser that you use on your Smartphone
2) You look for what you want to publish.
3) Copy the URL.
4) You return to the posting page of your LinkedIn page in the Smartphone application.
5) Paste the URL.
6) The preview is created.
7) Now you can delete the URL.
8) And now it only remains to do all the steps we've seen.

4.2.2.3 Posting images

4.2.2.3.1 Post an image

To publish a single image, we click on the camera icon, and we can do two things, take the photo right now to publish it, or upload it from the gallery of our Smartphone.

Under this, there are two icons, one to access the gallery and the blue to take the photo, now, I select the gallery icon and choose a photo.

When selecting a photo, at the bottom of the screen we see the Emoji gallery from LinkedIn.

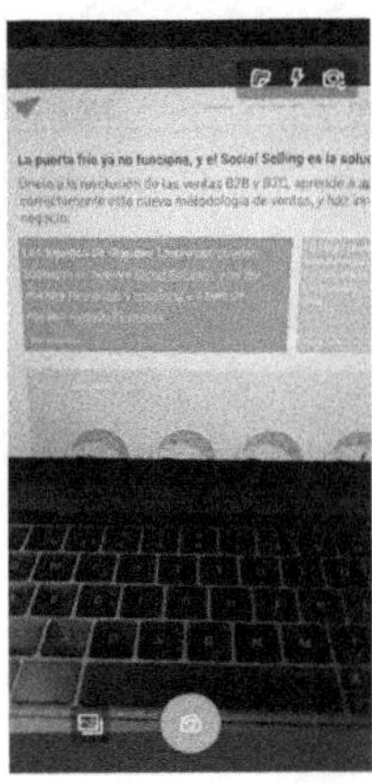

We select an Emoji and we can change it in size, rotate it and put where we want, we can also add several Emoji.

Another icon we have is the text icon that opens this menu, and allows us to write text, we can apply various effects.

And we can also change the text alignment, left, center and right.

4.2.2.3.2 Post multiple images

Just like on the computer we can publish several images and create a gallery, we can also do it from the Smartphone.

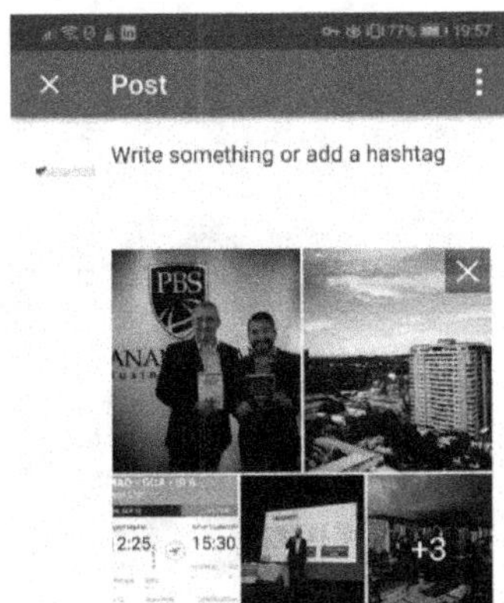

4.2.2.4 Post a video

Upon clicking the video camera icon, below the two main options, we see again the gallery icon, this time to post a video that we have saved on our Smartphone, and the red button to make a video now.

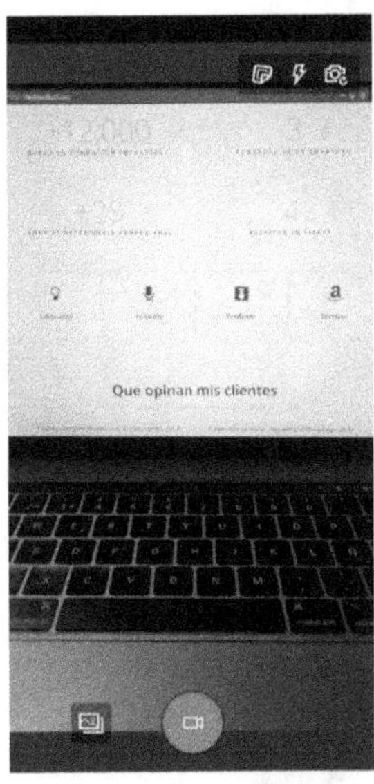

4.2.2.4.1 Post a video from the gallery

If we select the gallery option, we look for a video that we have saved, and we have the same options as when publishing photos, LinkedIn Emoji and we can add text.

4.2.2.4.2 Post a live video

If we select the red button to make the video immediately, and we can also put an Emoji in the video. In this video option we can not include text.

4.2.3 Post from Hootsuite

The social network management platform Hootsuite allows the programming of contents for publication in the company pages, Showcase Page and pages of universities.

Chapter 5

Viral content and Analytics

I this chapter we are going to look at one of the areas within the LinkedIn company page that is receiving the most changes, due to the importance it has to help us profile and improve our action plan.

We will be able to very deeply analyze what kind of content are the ones that work best on our page, which are generating more interactions and what kind, what is the profile of the professionals we are attracting to our page, with sector data, size of company, department, etc... and also a tool to analyze viral content.

The analytics section can be focused on analyzing the target users we want to reach, of the 575 million users, segmenting them, focusing only on the followers of our company page, or focusing on our employees.

Being able to develop different types of projects.

5.1 Content Suggestions

LinkedIn in the company pages, Showcase Page and Universities page, offers us the possibility of using a very powerful and also free of charge tool.

Would you like to know what exactly the most viral content is that is impacting your niche most right now? This is what Content Suggestions offers us.

In order to access this fabulous tool, we have to be administrators of the page and in the top menu we will see the option.

5.1.1 Setup Wizard

When you click on this menu option, the first thing it is going to ask us is if we want to filter the content to focus on our target customers.

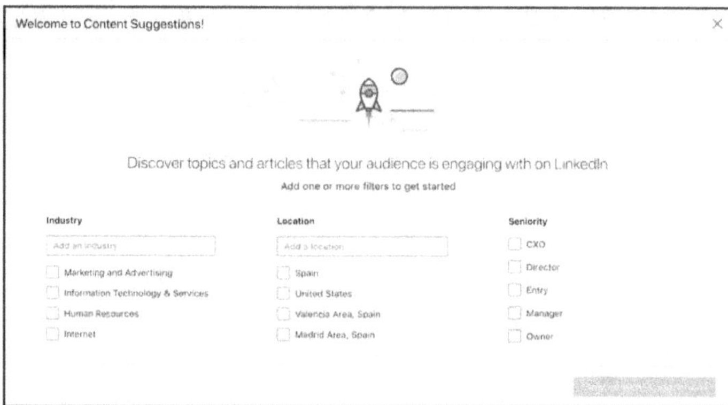

We can segment by "Industry", also indicate the "Location" and the level of experience or "Seniority" of the people to whom we want to impact.

In the first two options, we can write the ones we want and select them from the results, in the third "Seniority", only the options that it shows are available. Here I give you an example.

A very interesting point is that while you are configuring this filtering of the market you want to analyze, in the bottom left, we have in real time the amount of audience we are analyzing.

5.1.2 Results screen

Now we click the blue button "View content suggestions" and it will show us the most viral suggested content that is being seen, and with interactions by this group of professionals with the filter that we have created. And this is what that screen shows us.

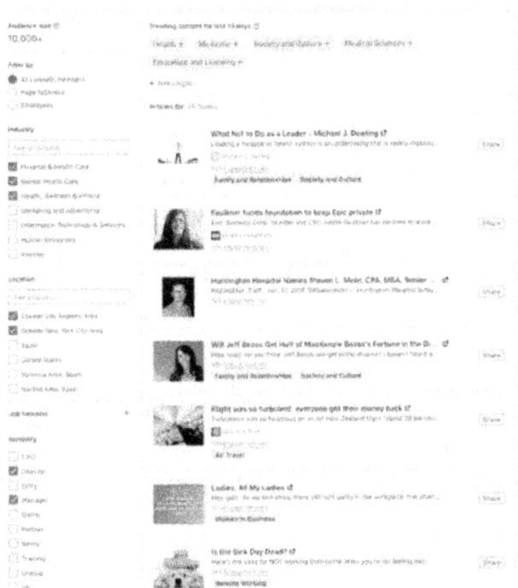

Now let's review the different parts of this screen. On the left side of the vertical, we have all the filtering options with more options available. In the upper right part it shows us more data about virality, and in the central part we already see the content.

5.1.3 Filtered by target members

We can see again the size of the audience in real time, and now it shows us an option that we did not have before, if we want to focus on it:

1) All LinkedIn members, this option allows us to analyze the entire LinkedIn user base worldwide, applying the filters that we have activated. Ideal for analysis of your sector, new markets you want to work in, to identify niches, and to see the interests of your potential customers.

2) Page followers, this allows us to focus only on the interests of the followers of our page. With this option we will be able to determine more clearly what the themes and types of content that interest our followers, allowing us to redesign our content strategy and adapt it better, to achieve greater attraction, consolidating more loyalty and interactions of followers.

3) Employees, with this option we focus exclusively on the interests of employees, a fabulous functionality that can be used by both marketing departments and human resources, to perform joint actions of employee loyalty and brand ambassador projects.

The other two filtering options "Industry" and "Location", work the same.

5.1.4 Filtered by Job function

In the wizard we saw, we did not have this option which allows us to define the function of the person, without needing to specify the title of his position, for example, we can filter by "Finance", because we want to see what related to health interests the people in that department.

Job function

Add a job function

☑ Finance

☐ Sales

☐ Other

☐ Information Technology

☐ Management

☐ Manufacturing

5.1.5 Filtered by Seniority

We had seen this option before, but now it shows us more options.

Seniority

☐ CXO

☑ Director

☐ Entry

☑ Manager

☐ Owner

☐ Partner

☐ Senior

☐ Training

☐ Unpaid

☐ VP

5.1.6 Filtered by theme

In the upper part of the screen, it gives us information about the trends of the contents that it is showing us, as we can see in the image below.

Regarding the search we have done, LinkedIn's Content Suggestions tool has determined a series of topics on which the content that it has shown us are based.

Now, what we can do is activate the ones we want and add others. Keep in mind, that the themes it shows you are in gray, because they are still deactivated, until you activate them.

Here you can see how I have activated these two, and at the moment of activating them, the contents shown are updated.

If we click on "+ Add a topic" we can write the topic that interests us and select it from the list.

Like this.

Leaving the filtering of the topics on which we want to focus, the contents that comply with all the filters that we have been applying appear.

5.1.7 Viral content

This is an example of the results, if you do exactly the same filters that I have done, the results will change, because they are in real time.

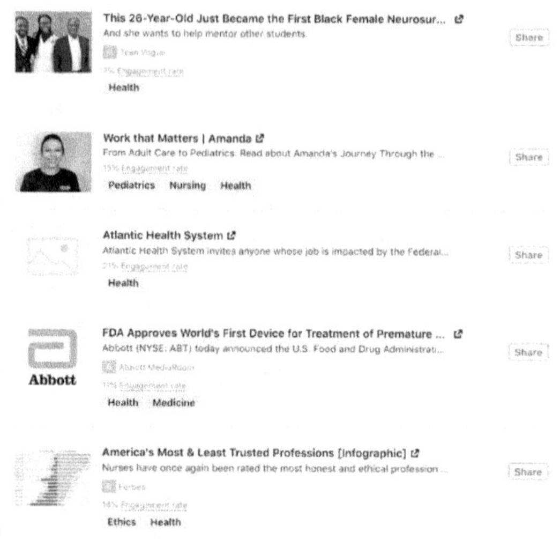

Analyzing the content, we can see on the left, a preview of the post, which is the image that will be seen if we share this content.

The title of the post is in bold, and below that, the subtitle.

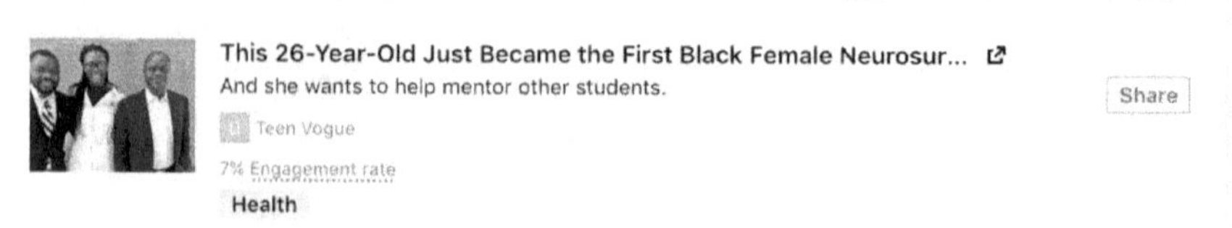

The name of the original medium of this post.

5.1.7.1 LinkedIn engagement formula

The level of engagement that this post has within LinkedIn.

7% Engagement rate

The formula that LinkedIn uses to calculate this value is this:

Engagement rate % = (Like + Comments + Share + Clicks + Follow) / (unique impressions for the selected audience)

Here we see another post with a different ratio, in this case 15% Engagement.

5.1.7.2 Post themes

The last option that appears in the content is of the themes that we have selected, to which this post belongs.

Health

5.1.7.3 Review the content

To make sure that the content is being shown to us, and thus decide if we want to share it, we can click on the image, on the black title or on the arrow on the right.

This 26-Year-Old Just Became the First Black Female Neurosur...

5.1.7.4 Share content

If we see this content as interesting for our target audience, we have the option to share it on our page by clicking on the blue "Share" button.

Share

When clicking on the button, the posting screen will appear; you can see how the name of my company appears, the post will not be done in your name, but you will publish it on your company's page.

I recommend that you do not publish the content like this, to achieve greater effectiveness, you need to write a text before it, in addition to adding # hashtags and if it is possible to use the @ to mention.

5.2 Analysis

Within the analysis tool we have three options.

1) Visitors, the people who visit our page, who may or may not be followers of the page.
2) Updates, the statistics of our publications, to see how they are working.
3) Followers, the statistics of the people who have clicked on the follow button of our page.

5.2.1 Analysis of visitors

Within the options to analyze the visitors of our page, we have three options.

We must use all this data and use the filters, to have a real picture of the results we are getting from our work on the page, and to decide that we should redesign our strategy.

5.2.1.1 Visitor highlights

In this section we see the total number of visits made to our page, unique visitors of the last 30 days, and we also see the comparison with respect to the previous 30 days.

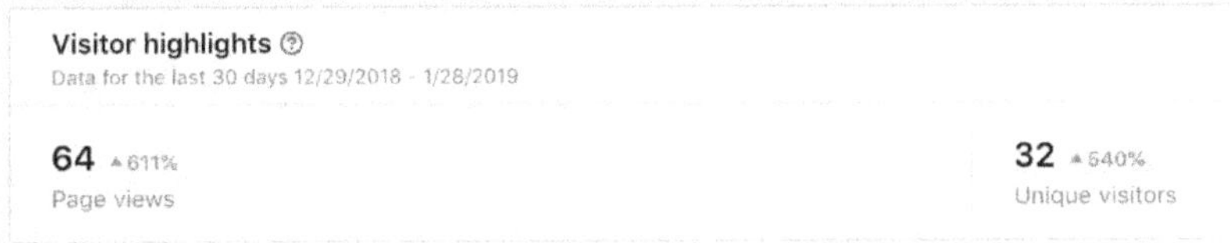

In this section we have no option to filter the range of dates.

In the right section we have a button to export the data, and we can filter them by date ranges.

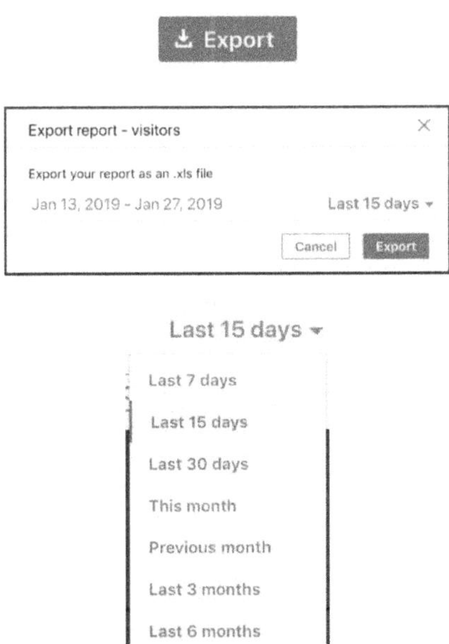

And we will download an Excel file with the data, to be able to treat them externally outside LinkedIn, or to save them as historical data, as you can see that you can not export data more than 6 months old.

5.2.1.2 Visitor metrics

This section is just below the previous one, and we can see and filter the page views and unique visitors, in more detail.

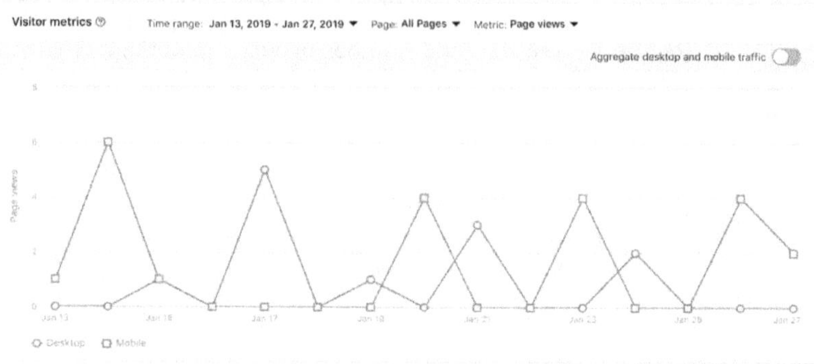

In the top right we can add the results of computer and mobile to see the total.

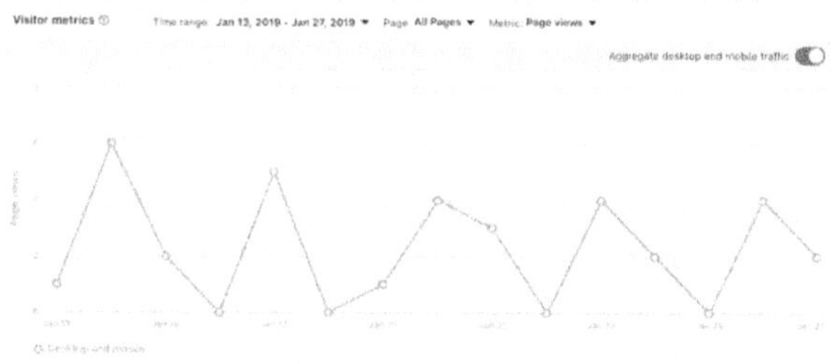

In this section if we have the option to filter by date ranges, default and manual.

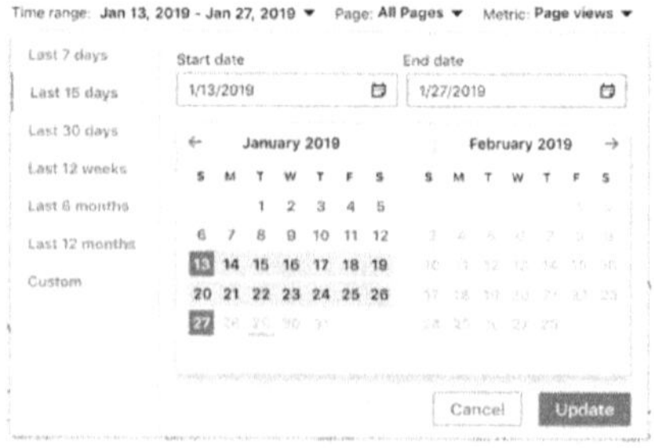

About the filtering we do and the data we want to see, page views or unique visitors, LinkedIn allows us to analyze the total of our page, or in each of the sections of our page.

Page business information, posts, jobs, employees, etc. ...

And we can make the graph show us visited pages or unique visitors.

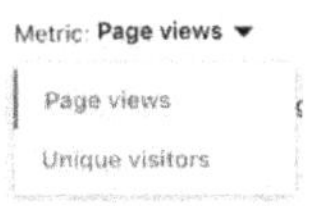

5.2.1.3 Visitor demographics

The last section of this screen is the demographics of our visitors.

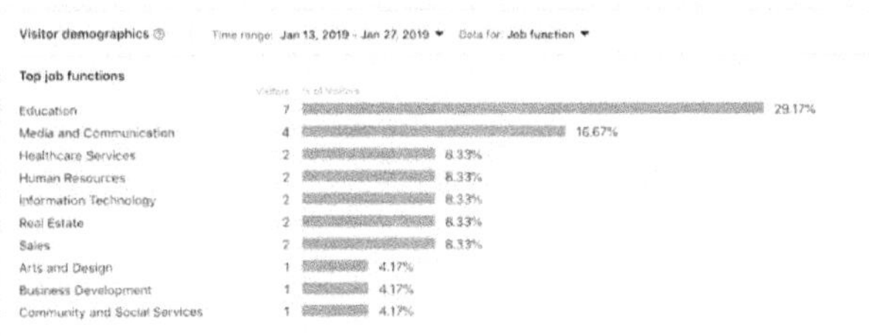

We can filter by dates and by these options.

5.2.1.3.1 Job function

Top job functions	Visitors	% of Visitors	
Education	7		29.17%
Media and Communication	4		16.67%
Healthcare Services	2		8.33%
Human Resources	2		8.33%
Information Technology	2		8.33%
Real Estate	2		8.33%
Sales	2		8.33%
Arts and Design	1		4.17%
Business Development	1		4.17%
Community and Social Services	1		4.17%

With this filtering option, we will see the visitor's position, we will see the corresponding department, sales, human resources, etc.

5.2.1.3.2 Location

Top locations	Visitors	% of Visitors	
Madrid Area, Spain	6		46.15%
Murcia Area, Spain	2		15.38%
Valencia Area, Spain	2		15.38%
San Francisco Bay Area	1		7.69%
Alacant Area, Spain	1		7.69%
Poznan, Greater Poland District, P...	1		7.69%

Here we will see what countries and cities we are receiving the visits from, to see if our work is creating the effect we seek to achieve.

5.2.1.3.3 Seniority

Top seniorities	Visitors	% of Visitors	
Senior	9		60%
Entry	6		40%

In this example only two come out, but more may appear, CXO, VP, Manager, Director, etc.

5.2.1.3.4 Industry

Visitor demographics	Time range: Jan 13, 2019 - Jan 27, 2019 ▼	Data for: Industry ▼

Top industries

	Visitors	% of Visitors
Primary/Secondary Education	4	22.22%
Education Management	3	16.67%
Civic & Social Organization	2	11.11%
Biotechnology	1	5.56%
Hospital & Health Care	1	5.56%
Leisure, Travel & Tourism	1	5.56%
Higher Education	1	5.56%
Public Relations and Communicati...	1	5.56%
Nonprofit Organization Managem...	1	5.56%
Translation and Localization	1	5.56%

These are the sectors to which the people who are visiting our page belong.

5.2.1.3.5 Company size

Visitor demographics	Time range: Jan 13, 2019 - Jan 27, 2019 ▼	Data for: Company size ▼

Top company sizes

	Visitors	% of Visitors
2 to 10 employees	3	21.43%
1,001 to 5,000 employees	3	21.43%
11 to 50 employees	2	14.29%
10,001+ employees	2	14.29%
51 to 200 employees	1	7.14%
201 to 500 employees	1	7.14%
501 to 1,000 employees	1	7.14%
5,001 to 10,000 employees	1	7.14%

And in this last option we see the sizes of our visitors' companies.

5.2.2 Analysis of updates

The second analysis option is about the effectiveness of the posts that we have made on our page.

Analytics ▼

Visitors

Updates

Followers

Here in the top right we also have the export button, and it works exactly as we have seen in the visitors.

5.2.2.1 Update highlights

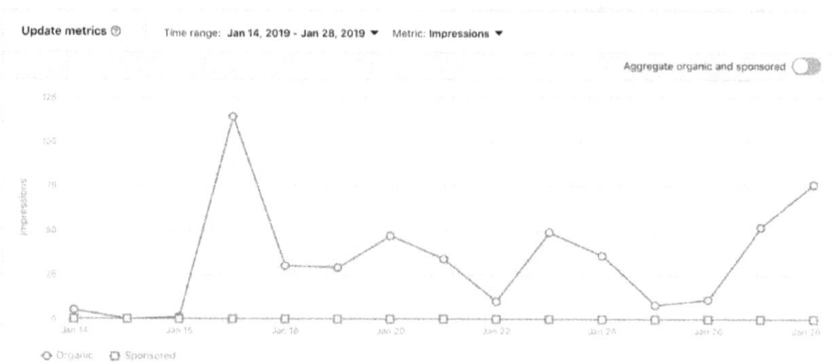

The first section that appears is the total data of the last 30 days of the likes that we have achieved, numbers of comments and sharing of our publications.

5.2.2.2 Update metrics

In this section we will see all this data. In the top right we can add the organic visualizations (blue color with circles) and those achieved with advertising (orange color with squares) on LinkedIn (sponsored).

- How many impressions we have achieved in total per day.
- Unique impressions.
- Interactions:
  - Number of clicks in the publications.
  - Likes.

o   Comments.
- The engagement rate.

To determine what an impression is, LinkedIn will do so taking into account that the post is at least 50% of the screen for at least 300 milliseconds, or by clicking on the post.

5.2.2.1.1 LinkedIn engagement rate formula

To calculate the engagement rate, LinkedIn uses this formula.

Engagement Rate = (Clicks + Likes + Comments + Shares + Followers) / Impressions

5.2.2.3 Update engagement

Update title	Posted by	Created	Impressions	Video views	Clicks	CTR	Likes	Comments	Shares	Foll
		1/23/2019	93	-	4	4.3%	3	0	2	
		1/17/2019	347	-	7	2.02%	11	1	1	
		12/13/2018	106	-	6	5.66%	1	0	0	
		11/29/2018	240	44	1	0.42%	3	0	0	
		11/28/2018	183	74	1	0.55%	3	0	1	
		11/27/2018	248	48	6	2.42%	3	0	0	
	David M Caldu...	11/23/2018	66	-	2	3.03%	1	0	0	
	David M Caldu...	11/30/2018	45	-	0	0%	0	0	0	
	David M Caldu...	11/13/2018	98	-	4	4.08%	3	0	0	

In this section we will see all the posts we have made, and the detail of each of them, who has published it, date, number of impressions, if it was a video, number of views, clicks, CTR, likes, comments and shares.

Impressions	Video views	Clicks	CTR	Likes	Comments	Shares	Follows	Engagement rate
93	-	4	4.3%	3	0	2	-	9.68%
347	-	7	2.02%	11	1	1	-	5.76%

And further to the right, we have how many followers we have achieved with each post and the engagement rate.

5.2.3 Analysis of followers

The last analysis section we have is to analyze the followers of our page.

In this section like the others, we also have the button to export the data.

5.2.3.1 Follower highlights

In these data are the total of followers that we have, and in the figure on the right, the new ones obtained in the last 30 days and the % of growth.

5.2.3.2 Follower metrics

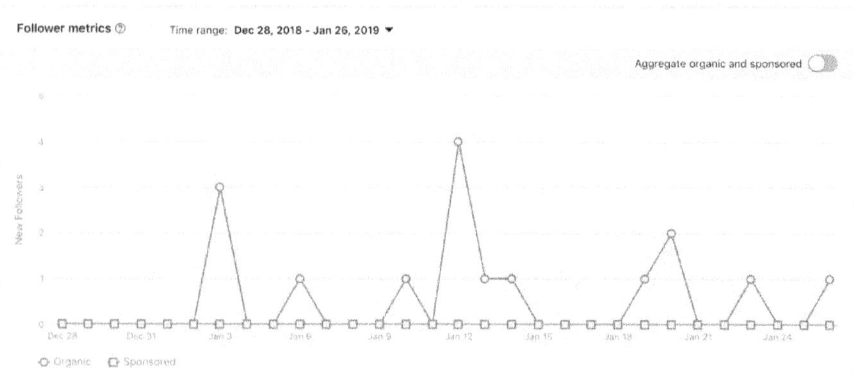

In the same way that we have seen before, we see the data of the followers that we have been getting divided into two values, by organic publications and by advertising (sponsored), and in the upper part we can add the two figures.

5.2.3.3 Follower Demographics

This screen is exactly the same as the other section that we had seen, but now with the volume of followers and demographic data it has, being able to filter by.

And here we see an example of the data shown to us.

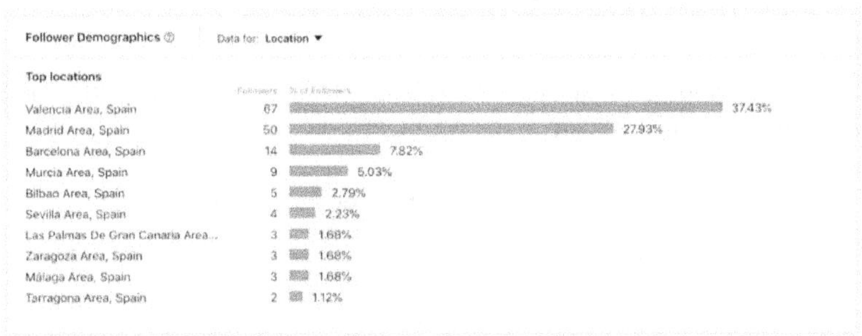

The formula to calculate the % is the following

Followers in this demographic group / Total follower with standardized demographics.

5.2.3.4 Companies to track

In this section we are shown other pages of similar companies, so that we can compare.

Company		Total followers	New followers	Number of updates	Engagement rate
Soluciona Facil	Your company	182	3	2	0%
		41	0	0	-
		1,601	-2	0	-
Microsoft		6,058,062	209,479	500	0.54%
		50	2	0	-
		337	14	0	-
		39	0	0	-
		18,019	701	4	0.51%
		4,960	120	18	1.29%

5.3 Activity

<table>
<tr><td>Page</td><td>Content Suggestions</td><td>Analytics ▼</td><td><u>Activity</u></td></tr>
</table>

The last option we have is "Activity", where we will see all the interactions that our posts have received.

In the left part of the screen we can filter by the type of interaction we want to see.

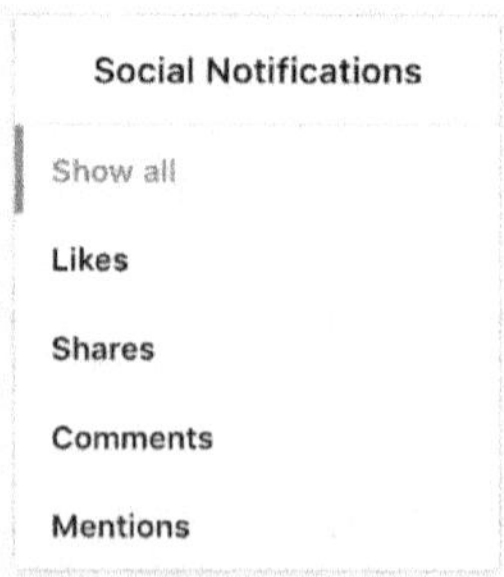

And here we see an example of how we will see those interactions.

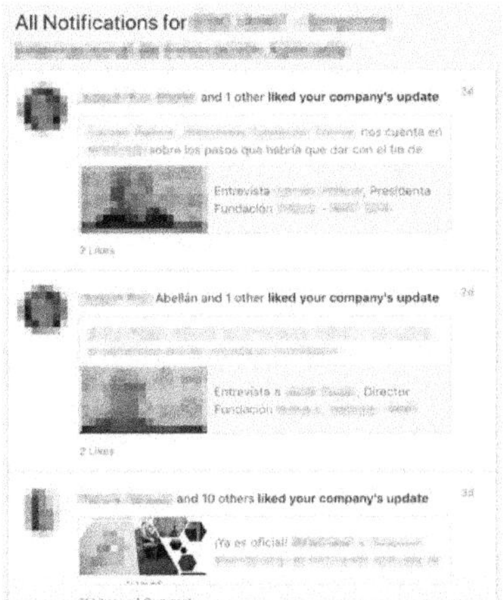

Chapter 6

Marketing Plan

To design our Marketing plan for the strategy that we will develop for our company on LinkedIn, we must plan a series of actions that will cover several areas of LinkedIn.

1) Company page and Showcase Pages.
2) LinkedIn Slideshare.
3) Posts on LinkedIn.
4) Advertising, sponsored content.
5) Advertising, sponsored InMail.
6) Advertising text type.

With this block of areas, we can develop a complete 360º plan that covers our LinkedIn in full, in this book we have seen point 1).

And now we are going to explain this point 1) seeing what kind of content we should publish, objectives, KPIs and a posting calendar.

6.1 Content to publish

6.1.1 Company news

A key point in our strategy is to give voice to the news that we want to be known about our company. I am not saying that you publish offers and promotions continuously, since you will convert your company page into an advertising brochure, and our main principal has to be to provide value.

We can post:

- New services that we offer at our company.

- New products that we add to our catalog.
- New features that we have incorporated into our existing products.
- Change of offices.
- Opening of new offices.
- Partnerships with other companies.
- Collaboration with NGOs.
- Incorporation of new professionals to our team.
- Show life within our company.

6.1.2 Blog content

Publishing content on the company's blog is one of the best strategies to position yourself at the SEO level, and what better way to disseminate it in a professional environment than to publish it on our corresponding company page or Showcase Page.

This can be done manually or through external tools, such as Hootsuite and Zappier, among others.

6.1.2.1 Automation with Hootsuite

Hootsuite allows you to post manually, schedule posts, and in the case that concerns us, automate them. To do this, we have to go to the top right menu, and when it is displayed, we select the option "Account & Settings".

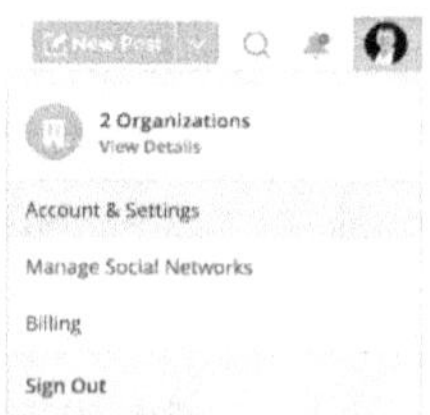

When selecting this option, this screen will appear.

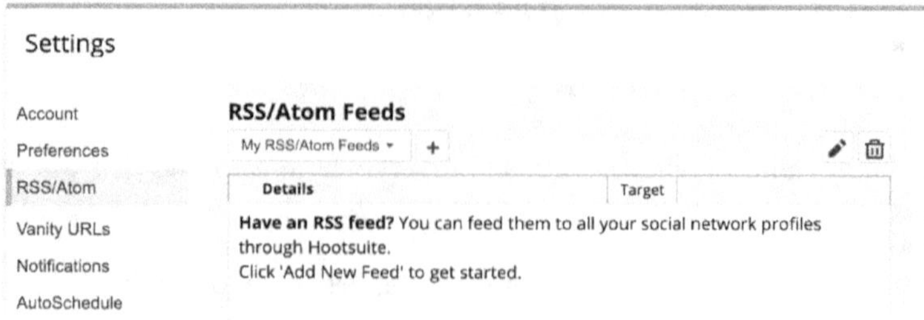

In the left part we have the options menu, and we select RSS / Atom, we will show the screen you are looking at and press the button with the + symbol that is in the center of the screen, in the upper part.

By clicking on the + we are shown this screen, I have filled in an example.

The first field to fill is "Feed URL", which is the Feed of your blog, if you are using Wordpress, it is your domain or your blog followed by / feed

The next thing that it asks us is where we want the new articles to be published (the previous ones at the time of the configuration are not published, only the new ones from now on), in my case I have selected the company's page on LinkedIn.

The next field "Check this feed for news posts every", I have indicated that every hour go to the company blog to see if there is a new post, and if there is one to post it.

The next drop-down is how many new articles you have to publish at the same time if there are several, I have told you only the latest.

And in the white box at the end, I added a text to include it in front of the articles when I published them, in my case "New post:". If you want you can leave it blank, so only the title of the article will appear without any text in front.

In the part of configuring the RSS feed, I want to tell you that almost everything is RSS, the Youtube channel of your company, etc. etc. etc. 

6.1.2.2 Automation with Zappier

Zappier is an application in the cloud, which allows us to connect different platforms and tools, and automate processes.

If you go to this address

https://zapier.com/apps/linkedin/integrations/wordpress

You will see the options that allow us to configure. In this example I show you how to connect your Wordpress blog with the company page on LinkedIn.

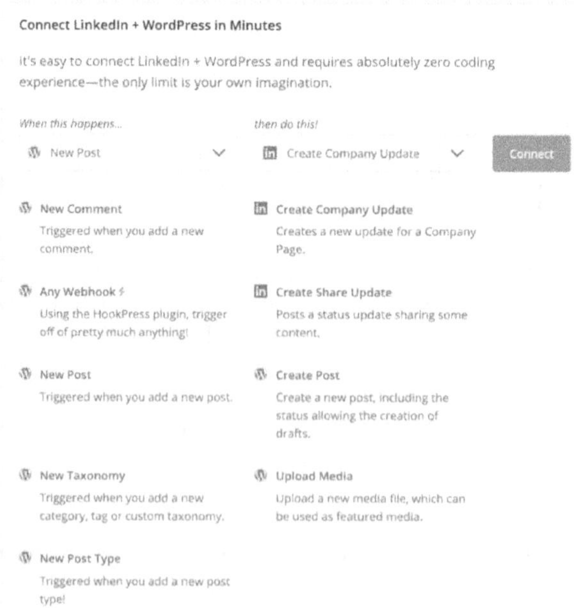

Connect LinkedIn + WordPress in Minutes

it's easy to connect LinkedIn + WordPress and requires absolutely zero coding experience—the only limit is your own imagination.

When this happens...	then do this!	
New Post	Create Company Update	Connect
New Comment Triggered when you add a new comment.	**Create Company Update** Creates a new update for a Company Page.	
Any Webhook Using the HookPress plugin, trigger off of pretty much anything!	**Create Share Update** Posts a status update sharing some content.	
New Post Triggered when you add a new post.	**Create Post** Create a new post, including the status allowing the creation of drafts.	
New Taxonomy Triggered when you add a new category, tag or custom taxonomy.	**Upload Media** Upload a new media file, which can be used as featured media.	
New Post Type Triggered when you add a new post type!		

If you use Tumblr as a platform to publish, here is how you can automate it https://zapier.com/apps/linkedin/integrations/tumblr

If you are a user of the Ghost platform, these are the integration options

https://zapier.com/apps/linkedin/integrations/ghost

6.1.3 News and industry research

If we want to maximize the visits to our company page, and get more followers, we can not focus exclusively on news related to our company, but we must open the view.

A good strategy is to provide value, posting news from our sector, and research carried out in our sector. This will allow us to post content of value that is still related to us.

The previous work that you are going to have to do here, is to identify and gather the sources of information that you consider relevant to your sector, to include them in the potential to post content.

A good idea to do this compilation is to talk with the managers and professionals of your company, so they tell you what sources are reported to be up to date in your sector.

6.1.4 Case studies and success stories

There is nothing more powerful than showing examples of other companies, to see what has worked for them, and so our potential customers identify with that case, by the type of company, by the company sector, because it is the same size, has the same problem, etc. and thus be able to generate Leads.

To publish the case studies, I recommend that you create a document template, with a visual style and sections, and that you create all of them with that template, to save a unified image.

6.1.5 Webinars

Webinars is a very good way to make segmented funnels to gather Leads. The issue that we have in the Webinar is the type of contact that will be registered.

When planning this type of action, the first thing to be clear is that it will not work if we are going to do one or two, we need to educate and accustom our audience to the idea that we regularly do webinars.

The next step is to make a list of topics that we are going to discuss, but the important thing is, not topics that interest you, but the question you have to ask is, what interests my Leads?

You must consider what day of the week is better, what week of the month, and what time, and duration, remember that we are directed to professionals and time is limited.

If you can also synchronize several tools to optimize your time, much better, I'll explain how I do it as an example.

I work with the Zoho CRM https://www.solucionafacil.es/zoho/ you can register here for free.

Registration forms for the events I make with Zoho Forms, when people register, they are automatically registered in the CRM.

For the management of webinars, schedules, what will be discussed, I use Zoho Backstage, which I also have it automatically integrated with Zoho Forms and Zoho CRM.

And with Zoho Meeting is how I do the Webinar and I record it, and as you can imagine, I integrate it with all the other tools. The idea is to save time.

6.1.6 Statistics and Infographics

Statistical data is a type of content that works very well, since they are data that give us trends that we can apply. The next step is to convert it or look for it in Infographics, which allows us to collect a lot of data in a single image.

Here is an example of an infographic on Twitter

https://www.slideshare.net/davidmcalduch/el-poder-oculto-de-twitter-por-davidmcalduch-twitter-spain-twitteradses

To make infographics you can use tools like:

- Canva.com
- Piktochart.com
- Visme.co

6.1.7 Downloadable PDFs and Guides

Creating downloadable guides is also a good practice, offering the download in exchange for people's data. It is a type of funnel that only those who are interested in that content will fill in the data to download it.

I use Zoho Forms, and when filling out the data, you will automatically be sent an email with the link of the Guide to download it, or you can send it as an attachment, and automatically the data filled in by the person are registered within Zoho CRM.

I give you two examples here:

- Free SSI Guide for what to do and how to increase it

https://www.linkedin.com/feed/update/urn:li:activity:6469967439567351808

- Free Social Selling Guide

https://forms.zoho.com/virtualoffice5461/form/GuiaSocialSellingSolucionaFacil

6.1.8 Video Marketing

For me to explain here all the dynamics of Video Marketing, how to do it, etc. we would occupy a whole book, so I give you some data and a powerful tool for you to do.

90% of customers made the decision to buy when watching videos, and 64% say that after watching a video they are more willing to buy.

- Forbes

Currently it is the type of content that generates more engagement. Here is the platform that I use to generate videos for my clients and for my company.

www.solucionafacil.es/video

Videos increase conversions by 80%.

- Unbounce

In addition, it allows you to create videos automatically from your data sources, Excel, Database, create a video of each post, a video of each product in your eCommerce, a video for each customer personalized with your name, etc.

Video creators generate 66% more qualified leads per year.

- Aberdeen

6.2 KPIs

The analytics part we have already seen, and here I put some of the KPIs that I recommend that you measure:

- Followers of the pages
- Clicks on posts
- Engagement
- Questions
- Leads
- Records to events
- Downloads of PDFs

6.3 Posting calendar

At this point I just want to highlight, that for the company page to work, it is necessary to dedicate a lot of work, and make a large number of monthly posts.

If you want the page to be active, you will need at least 20 posts per month, and if you have it as a priority to maximize it, you will have to increase that effort up to 3 publications per day.

As you can see, it is not a minor volume, so you will have to make it truly a priority for the company, and thus be able to allocate the necessary human and material resources to make it work.

Chapter 7

Common problems and their solutions

7.1 Delete a page

To delete a page, you have to follow these steps; there is no way to undo the deletion once it has been confirmed.

1) You must have Administrator permissions
2) Go to the company page, and in the top right you have the "Admin tools" menu and select the last option "Deactivate Company Page".

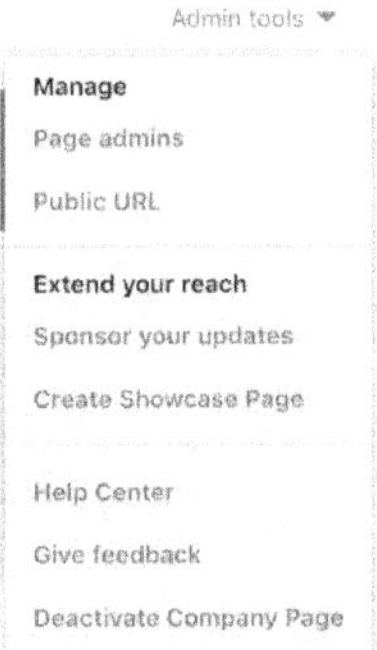

3) This notice will appear, that once we have done this action, there is no turning back.

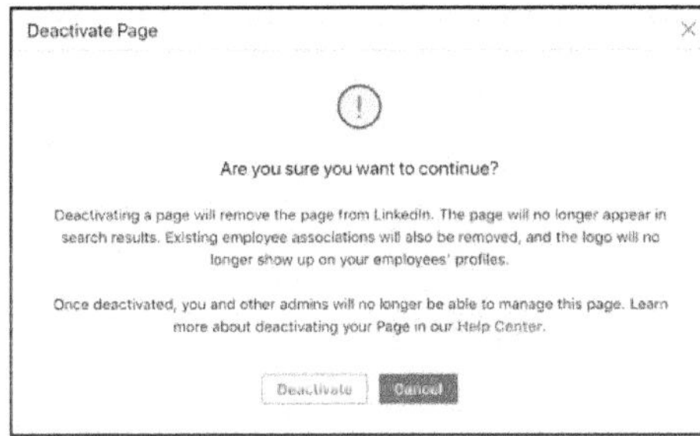

4) 4) And pressing "Deactivate" deletes the page and shows this confirmation.

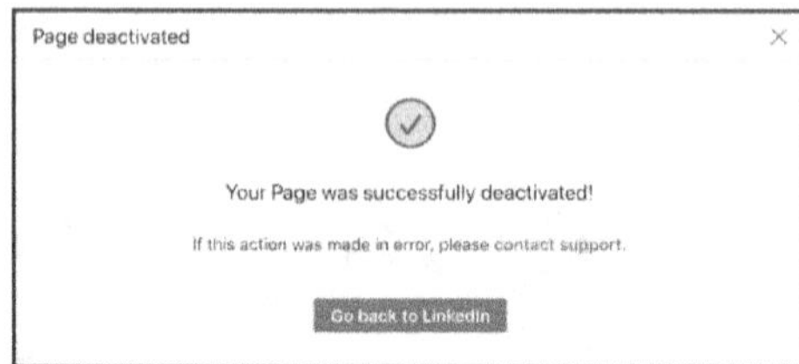

When carrying out the process from within the page, although it is deleted, you can still see it on your screen, at the moment you update the browser, you will see that it gives you an error because you can not find it anymore.

7.2 Delete a person as an employee

It may happen that a person puts in their profile, that they work or has worked for your company or university. If it is false, you can contact LinkedIn to remove that professional profile reference to your page and disappear as an employee or former employee.

To do this you must fill in this form

https://linkedin.com/help/linkedin/ask/TS-NFPI

Chapter 8

Final tips

Ihope you have followed my advice, and applied what we have seen in the book. If you have, you can now use this book, as a reference book.

If you liked this book, I encourage you to give your opinion on Amazon https://www.amazon.com/author/davidmcalduch

And, if you want to continue advancing in your knowledge, you can continue with the rest of the books in the series: https://thekeysof.com/linkedin

www.ingramcontent.com/pod-product-compliance
Lightning Source LLC
Chambersburg PA
CBHW071453030726
47593CB00003B/986